P9-DEA-966

Prayer Voices

Prayer Voices

A Popular Theology of Prayer

Edited by H. Robert Cowles
and K. Neill Foster

CHRISTIAN PUBLICATIONS
CAMP HILL, PENNSYLVANIA

Christian Publications
3825 Hartzdale Drive, Camp Hill, PA 17011

The mark of ❧ vibrant faith

ISBN: 0–87509–544–5
LOC Card Catalog Number: 93–071374
© 1993 by Christian Publications
All rights reserved
Printed in the United States of America

93 94 95 96 97 5 4 3 2 1

Unless otherwise indicated, Scripture taken
from the HOLY BIBLE: NEW
INTERNATIONAL VERSION®. ©1973, 1978,
1984 by the International Bible Society.
Used by permission of Zondervan Publishing House.
All rights reserved.

Dedication

To our retired workers and friends
who pray without ceasing
for The Christian and Missionary Alliance.

Who may ascend the hill of the LORD?
Who may stand in his holy place?
He who has clean hands and a pure heart,
who does not lift up his soul to an idol
or swear by what is false.
(Psalm 24:3–4)

Create in me a pure heart, O God,
and renew a steadfast spirit within me.
Do not cast me from your presence
or take your Holy Spirit from me.
Restore to me the joy of your salvation
and grant me a willing spirit, to sustain me.
Then I will teach transgressors your ways,
and sinners will turn back to you.
(Psalm 51:10–13)

If I had cherished sin in my heart,
the Lord would not have listened.
(Psalm 66:18)

Contents

Preface

Prayer Voices is a book that called itself into being. With an observable and increasing desire to give ourselves over to prayer evident everywhere in The Christian and Missionary Alliance—and alongside a new missionary thrust into Russia—there has been no doubt at Christian Publications that a book was in order.

Participants cooperated with a tight deadline to get text in on time. H. Robert Cowles pitched heartily into the editing process and the pleasant result is a popular theology focused on what various leaders in our fellowship are saying about prayer!

The themes are varied but, like threads of fabric, they create a pattern of present reality—this is the way we are praying and this is what we are praying about.

K. Neill Foster
Easter 1993

Principles
of
Prayer

	Pray
CHAPTER	**First**
1	

by David L. Rambo

THIS IS THE LAST DECADE of the last century of what is probably the last full millennium this planet will ever know. As such, it is seeing a uniquely religious phenomenon: a proliferation of organizations with strategies to achieve great things for God within the next seven years.

The phenomenon has become known as the "AD 2000 Movement." One delegate to the International Congress on World Evangelization in Manila defined it as "a worldwide chorus, or a symphony orchestra, conducted by God to fulfill the Great Commission by the end of the century." He predicted that out of the congress in Manila would come 50 national-level AD 2000 projects and that by 1995 there would be 100.

On an even grander scale, international organizations like World Evangelical Fellowship, Lausanne Congress and AD 2000 have global plans leading up to the end of the century. Bold and aggressive, even overlapping and sometimes competitive, their programs reflect a "can-do" spirit of confidence that evangelizing the world can be realized in a few years.

Whistle-Blowing Time

Yet despite all the fanfare of convocations and busyness of committees, a haunting question persists. Where is the engine to make these big plans work? Something deep inside me suggests that we are talking big, but is there enough power in the church to deliver the goods?

What seems missing in the bewildering maze of programs is an emphasis on prayer equal to the strong reliance on action—as if strategy, management and goals are what really count. I see little groundswell of prayer paralleling in scope or enthusiasm the aspirations of these broad movements.

Perhaps it's time to blow the whistle. Do we really think we can expect so much from God with so little prayer?

In fact, the decline of interest in prayer in evangelical circles has become a major problem. The midweek prayer meeting in many churches is traveling the same downhill road as the Sunday evening service. Both are threatened species with few functional substitutes in sight.

Even in Alliance churches, if we are able to

muster 20 or even 10 percent of our Sunday morning congregation for the midweek service, we are fortunate. A few decades ago, evangelicals scorned mainline churches for their one-service weekly schedules. Now we are fast headed in the same direction, especially with regard to corporate prayer.

Is enthusiasm for world evangelization and silence on prayer suggesting that maybe the church can do this one on its own?

Cry of Helplessness

One of the concurrent themes of the 1993 General Council is *Pray First*. These two words put all our ambitious plans of expanding mission, plotting church growth, promoting evangelism and reaching unreached peoples into proper perspective.

When Christ surveyed the crowds following Him like a leaderless mass of confused and desperate people needing every kind of help, He had compassion on them. Telling His disciples to do something about their need, He likened the crowds to a field ripe for harvest. But His first command was not to form a work crew, or plot a master grid for the fields, or dash out and start reaping. Instead, He urged them, "Ask the Lord of the harvest . . ." (Matthew 9:38).

Prayer is the engine seriously needed yet obviously lacking in many efforts by the church in its driving ambition to accomplish so much by the end of this decade. Unless there is a crying out to God for help equal to or surpassing the energy and resources committed to our grand plans, we are doomed to failure and rightly so. The Lord said, in essence, "Pray first."

We need to be careful, however, that prayer does not become simply another tool to achieve our goals. This would amount to little more than an effort to manipulate God to assure success on our terms—a repugnant idea.

I am sure the Lord Jesus had something else in mind when He told His followers first to "Ask the Lord of the harvest. . . ." Surveying the crowds of people that carpeted the hillsides and crowded the roads like a microcosm of humanity, He knew the disciples were no match for the masses. The human needs pressing in on them were far too complex and deep for them to resolve. They were as helpless to help the crowds as the crowds were powerless to save themselves.

O. Hallesby defined prayer as the ultimate cry of helplessness. He wrote,

This is unquestionably the first and the surest indication of a praying heart. As far as I can see, prayer has been ordained only for the helpless. . . . Prayer and helplessness are inseparable. Only he who is helpless can truly pray.

That is precisely what the disciples needed to do before they could be of any use to the Lord. And we can do no better.

A cursory glance at some of the factors militating against evangelization of the world by AD 2000 or anytime soon should convince us of our helplessness:

• Most of the world's people—a staggering 83 percent—yet to be reached with the gospel live in countries where traditional missionary work and evangelism are impossible.

• Creeping universalism in the evangelical community is undermining one of the prime reasons for missions, i.e., that people without knowledge of Christ are lost.

• The gospel is being increasingly confronted by militant world religions such as Islam with its deep pockets of petrodollars and Hinduism with its newly awakened nationalism.

• The decline of economic power in North America weakens financial support for the local church, drains dollars from mission budgets, and in general hobbles the primary source of mission personnel and resources among the nations.

These are a few factors in the long line of roadblocks to the Great Commission. They should convince us that no amount of goal-managed organization and global strategy will be adequate. "Pray First" becomes an agonizing recognition that without God our very best efforts will fall short.

Opening for Help

"Pray First" does more than acknowledge our total inability to do God's work. When deeply and sincerely expressed, it opens the door for Him to act.

This serious spiritual exercise is far removed from the perfunctory praying that often characterizes the opening of church services and business meetings. God is very much the gentleman: He will not intrude where not wanted or merely invited as a formality.

The quality of prayer needed is brought out by a closer examination of the verb used in "Ask the Lord of the harvest . . ." (Matthew 9:38). The Greek word *deomai* means "to beg." It expresses intensity, almost a sense of desperation. It is used sparingly in the New Testament.

The verb is also found in an event recorded in Acts at the time when the Jerusalem believers were being repressed severely by Jewish authorities and Peter had been arrested. After being miraculously delivered from prison, he met with others for some serious praying. "After they prayed [*deomai*], the place where they were meeting was shaken. And they were all filled with the Holy Spirit and spoke the word of God boldly" (Acts 4:31).

The same form of the verb has a tone of desperation later in Acts. Peter had severely rebuked Simon the Sorcerer for thinking he could buy the gift of anointing people with the Spirit. Terrified at the thought of divine punishment, Simon begged the apostles, "Pray [*deomai*] to the Lord for me so that nothing you have said may happen to me" (Acts 8:24).

Perhaps the most revealing use of the verb appears in Paul's exalted view of the ministry of reconciliation: "We are therefore Christ's ambassadors, as though God were making his appeal through us. We implore [*deomai*] you on Christ's behalf: Be reconciled to God" (2 Corinthians 5:20).

What could be more wholehearted than the intensity of Christ's own love, more compelling than the urgency of Christ's own concern, that people find peace with God! This is the level of seriousness with which we should ask the Lord of the harvest for help in our witness to the world.

Urgency. Intensity. Helplessness to the point of desperation. When these characterize our prayer preparation for doing God's work, we will open the door for God to bless our efforts beyond anything we can imagine. Resistance to the gospel will be swept away, the powers of darkness shackled. Miracles will punctuate our witness. Spoken truth will be vested with authority. Lives will be magnificently transformed. Christ will be lifted up in winsome glory.

All this and more will follow our efforts to evangelize the world—but only when we preface our activity with a cry of helplessness to the point of desperation and with an urgent plea for help that sets God free to work as He pleases.

Collective Clout

"Pray First" is a marvelous way to bring people together to achieve collectively what they could not do individually. It is no coincidence that the Early Church's rapid expansion, turning the world on its head, began with a prayer meeting in Jerusalem.

When Jesus' followers returned to the city after witnessing His ascension into heaven, "they all joined together constantly in prayer." And shortly after, "when the day of Pentecost came, they were all together in one place" (Acts 1:14, 2:1).

Together in the same place at the same time to pray about the same thing. How wonderful then, how rare now!

The worth of any movement or organization lies in its vision and values, not its structure. The cohesion in a mission-driven church like The Christian and Missionary Alliance is generated and reinforced through prayer. This principle goes all the way back to the church in Antioch. Before Christians in Antioch fielded the very first missionary team of the New Testament era, they fasted and prayed, and then sent off Barnabas and Paul (Acts 13:3). The pattern has not changed.

This issue is more than an academic exercise for the Alliance. As I write, the Division of Overseas Ministries is mobilizing personnel and resources for a major church-planting mission in Russia.

The decision comes at a time when large numbers of Russians are turning to Christ but have no church home where they can be nurtured. Parachurch groups, realizing amazing results in Russia through evangelistic efforts, are urging the Alliance, widely respected for its focus on planting churches, to come and preserve the gains they are making.

But, in the familiar words of the apostle Paul, ". . . a great door for effective work has been opened . . . and there are many who oppose . . ." (1 Corinthians 16:9).

For over 70 years, the spiritual powers of darkness have had free reign through an atheistic government. They will not easily or quickly relinquish their domination over a vast and populous nation. False cults and eastern religions are already hard at work. They are meeting with impressive response from people searching for something—anything—spiritual to fill the void left by their fallen ideological god, Communism.

The only way an Alliance mission in Russia is

going to establish viable and evangelistic churches is through a higher level of prayer than we presently know in our Alliance churches. Our excellent organization and strategy, our long history and rich background of experience, our faithful giving people will not be enough.

Only through prayer, the cry of helplessness— only through prayer, the opening for God to work—only through prayer, the collective clout of a people united in vision and values, will the mission to Russia prosper.

An Individual Matter

What is true for "Pray First" in reference to strategies and organizations is equally true for individuals. The cry of helplessness sets God free to reshape us in the image of His Son. This truth lies at the heart of Paul's seeming contradiction, "When I am weak, then I am strong" (2 Corinthians 12:10).

Whether the personal need is for renewal or healing or guidance or whatever, the same principle applies: "Pray First." It is the ultimate confession of our weakness and confidence in God's power.

In the following chapters of this book, you will find writers touching on different aspects of prayer, ranging from specialized "Warfare Praying," to collective "Pray about Everything," from personal "Prayer for Healing," to general "Pray for Israel."

The whole exercise of prayer may seem daunting

in its difficulty and complexity. But the only way to learn how is to start doing it. This language of the spirit may have to begin with infantile gurgles and gasps, yet those who persevere will learn eventually to speak the language of prayer with heavenly tones and earthly power.

And in the process of learning this new language, we have the best help possible: ". . . the Spirit helps us in our weakness. We do not know what we ought to pray for, but the Spirit himself intercedes for us with groans that words cannot express" (Romans 8:26).

In Conclusion . . .

Thank God for evidences of a trans-denominational prayer network gaining momentum across the nation. It is a grassroots movement, not an operation planned in boardrooms or strategy huddles.

Bands of believers ranging from religious leaders at the top to humble believers in local churches across a broad spectrum gather without fanfare or rigid programs. They pray and then disperse, spiritually invigorated and their work as well. Herein lies the true hope for reviving the Church and evangelizing the world.

Will the Alliance be part of this? There are traces of concern becoming visible at Council time and among a small but growing number of Alliance workers and laymen.

Although currently like a cloud the size of a man's hand on the horizon, this movement has the potential of becoming the prime source of power and blessing among our churches. I pray that it will.

Dr. David L. Rambo is President of The Christian and Missionary Alliance in the United States.

CHAPTER	Praying
2	Like Jesus

by Maurice R. Irvin

A HYMN BY JAMES MONTGOMERY says, "Prayer is the Christian's vital breath, the Christian's native air." That statement is entirely true if we judge the nature of true Christian experience by the example of Jesus. It was entirely true of Him that prayer was His vital breath, His native air. And if we are to be like Christ, we must be people whose lives are immersed in prayer.

The four accounts of Jesus' life in the first four books of the New Testament contain some 27 different references to prayers offered by Jesus on at least 17 different occasions. In addition, these books contain a number of incidental references that say "Jesus blessed them" or "Jesus gave thanks." Looking at all these passages, I want to consider when Jesus prayed, how Jesus prayed and why Jesus prayed. And by all this I want us to discover from the example of Jesus what ought to be the pattern of our lives.

I simply turn the pages of the New Testament to

observe *when* our Lord engaged in prayer. Interestingly, by far the largest number of references to Jesus' prayer life are in Luke.

But I begin with Matthew. And I note an outburst of praise in Matthew 12:25–27 and that in Matthew 14 Jesus prayed just before He began to break the five loaves and two fishes to multiply this miraculously into enough food to feed more than 5,000 people. Shortly after this, Jesus went into a mountain apart to pray. Matthew 26 records the intercession of Jesus in the Garden of Gethsemane, and Matthew 27:46 reports one of the three cries of prayer Jesus uttered from the cross.

In Mark we are told in 1:35 that before one day of very busy ministry to people with all kinds of needs, Jesus rose up long before dawn and went out to a solitary place and prayed there. Mark also records the prayer of Jesus at the feeding of the 5,000 and that afterward He retired to a mountain to pray. Mark 7:34 reports that Jesus prayed as He healed a man who was deaf and dumb. Mark 14 also describes Jesus' session with His Father in Gethsemane, and Mark 15:34 refers to one of the outcries of prayer from the cross.

In Luke we learn from 3:21 that Jesus prayed when He was baptized, from 5:16 that He withdrew to a wilderness area to pray and from 6:12 that He spent all night on a mountain praying. Luke 10:21–22 records a prayer of praise. In Luke we are also told that He prayed at the feeding of the 5,000 and afterward. Luke alone tells us that Jesus was praying when He was transfigured before Peter, James and John, and that it was immediately after they saw Jesus at prayer that the disciples said, "Lord, teach us to pray." In Luke 22:32 Jesus said to Peter, "I have prayed for you." Luke 22 records Jesus praying in Gethsemane, and Luke 23 reports two utterances of prayer from the cross.

The Gospel of John also tells us that Jesus prayed over the food for the 5,000. Additionally, John 11:41 depicts Jesus in prayer at the tomb of Lazarus, and John 12:27–28 indicates that Jesus prayed when certain Greeks came seeking Him. Finally, Jesus prayed the great prayer for His people in John 17.

The Conclusions

What conclusions can we draw from these Scriptures? First, they indicate conclusively that Jesus prayed often. Even these 25 or so passages do not record every occasion on which He communicated with His Father. They simply illustrate what evidently was going on constantly throughout His lifetime. Jesus prayed often.

These Scriptures also indicate that Jesus prayed regularly. Several of the passages that describe particular instances of prayer, especially times of prayer in the morning and at night, imply that this was part of a pattern for Jesus, something He did repeatedly. I am convinced that Jesus prayed regularly.

We have no right to think of ourselves as people who are like Jesus unless we pray regularly and pray often. It is entirely incongruous that any of us should claim to be His followers if prayer is not an important part of our lives as it was for His.

But something more ought to be observed about when Jesus prayed. He also prayed instantly and specially when the situation demanded it. He prayed at the times of great events in His life—at His baptism, at His transfiguration, when facing the cross, from the cross. He prayed to summon power from heaven for special work He needed to do, to feed the 5,000, to heal the deaf-mute, to raise Lazarus from the dead. He prayed at once for people in special need—for His followers just before He was arrested and taken to the cross, especially for Peter, and for those who nailed Him to the cross. Evidently, the first recourse of Jesus in any situation of stress or need was to pray.

We should learn from the prayer life of Jesus not only to pray regularly and often, but to look toward heaven at every crisis and confrontation with need.

Some time ago, I read of an assault on the summit of Mt. Everest with what at that time was a new approach by a mountain climbing expedition. Men within that group worked in teams, and each member of a team was equipped with a radio so that he could keep in touch with the others. The article said that a vital part of the success of that team was the instant communications between the members upon every development, danger or difficulty encountered. And no doubt, success in Christian living depends upon instant communication with God at every difficulty and need we encounter. The example of Jesus indicates this.

How He Prayed

Looking at all these passages that describe His performance, what can we conclude concerning *the manner* of Jesus' praying?

First, some of the prayers of Jesus were as simple and as brief as a greeting between old friends, as a casual telephone conversation, as an order placed with the local drug store. I do not mean that Jesus was ever insincere. Rather, I am emphasizing the simplicity with which He sometimes prayed.

At His baptism Jesus apparently quickly committed Himself to God. His prayer on that occasion was so inconspicuous that two of the three Gospels that describe His baptism fail to mention that Jesus prayed. Before He fed the 5,000 Jesus quietly gave thanks to God. Though He had wept in grief over the death of Lazarus, Jesus, in John 11:41–42, spoke to God a simple prayer before He raised Lazarus from the dead. Obviously prayer was, at times, for Jesus as natural as breathing in and breathing out, as spontaneous as a smile, as simple as the humming of a familiar song.

Prayer also should sometimes be this way for us. Our thoughts should be so frequently on the Lord, our relationship with Him so personal, our sense of dependence on Him so constant, that we simply pray again and again about things that are going on around us in quiet, uncomplicated conversations with our Lord.

I note with you also, however, that at other times Jesus prayed, even though still briefly, with great emotion and agitation of soul. Hebrews 5:7 says that in the days of His flesh Jesus offered up prayers and supplications with strong crying and tears. Such praying is described in several passages in the Gospels.

When certain Greeks were seeking Jesus in John 12, Jesus was deeply moved. He said, "Now is my soul troubled." And then Jesus prayed with what was evidently deep agony of soul. Luke tells us that when Jesus prayed in Gethsemane His agitation was so intense, His feelings so moved, that His sweat was as great drops of blood falling to the ground. And, of course, at least two of the expressions of prayer from the cross were uttered in great anguish or in great intensity of spirit.

If then, we pray like Jesus, there will be times when we are deeply moved and intensely concerned in prayer. A dimension in our prayer life is missing if we never are provoked in intercession to tears, to deep yearnings, to intense concern. I must admit with some shame that there used to be times more often than now when I was deeply burdened in prayer, when I cried out with inner groaning to God, when I could not do other things because my spirit was so engaged by concern. The example of Jesus should call us back to times of intense, fervent prayer.

Protracted Seasons

Another aspect of Jesus' manner of praying should be considered. Jesus often spent protracted periods in prayer. I asked a Bible study group one evening, "Do you find it better to have an extended time of prayer with God in the mornings, when you first get up, or in the evenings, before retiral?" One woman in the group said, "Pastor, I don't need a special time in the morning or at night. I pray at the sink while I'm washing dishes. I pray as I drive the car to the store. I pray while I'm running the vacuum sweeper." And obviously, it is possible and Christlike to pray that way. But I believe that we fool ourselves if we think that this kind of praying is enough. Jesus also spent extended time in prayer alone, in quiet places and at unusual hours so that He was not distracted, interrupted or disturbed. And we ought to follow His example in this. Luke 6:2 says that Jesus went out into a mountain and continued all night in prayer to God. Mark 1:35 informs us, "In the morning, a great while before day, He rose up and went out into a mountain and continued all night in prayer to God." And these are but two of several such references in the Gospels.

Jesus was not a religious hermit who, because He had nothing else to do, could afford the time for extended periods of prayer. Jesus lived, as one writer puts it, "an incredibly busy life." He was constantly preaching, teaching, casting out demons, healing individuals or large groups of people, and He always was surrounded by excited, jostling, seething multitudes. But despite His busyness, He took time for extended periods of prayer. In fact, James G.S. Thomson suggests that "the harder Christ's days, the longer His prayer time; the busier He was, the greater His insistence on the practice of the presence of His Father."

Most Christians find 20 minutes of nothing but prayer a long time. Our minds wander or we fall asleep when we attempt long sessions of prayer alone. The use of a written prayer list can help us keep our minds on what we ought to be praying about. Changing postures can help keep us awake. Praying aloud even though we are alone may help some of us.

Still, protracted times of prayer are not easy. Not many Christians are going to begin at once spending hours at a time in extended intercession. But we should spend some periods of uninterrupted, concentrated times with God. And a developing prayer life might well lead us into practices closer and closer to those of Christ in this respect. When we think of ourselves as striving after Christlikeness, let us remember that Jesus often spent long periods alone in prayer with the Father.

Why Jesus Prayed

A third consideration deserves our attention. Looking at all the verses that describe Jesus' activities in this regard, I ask, *"What did He accomplish in prayer?"* And there are at least four answers to that question.

First, Jesus prayed to give thanks to God. Matthew 1:25–27 and Luke 10:21–22 record an occasion when Jesus simply cried out, "I thank Thee, O Father, Lord of heaven and earth." His prayer at the grave of Lazarus was a prayer of thanksgiving. The prayer He expressed at the feeding of the 5,000 was a prayer of thanksgiving. Part of the time Jesus prayed just to give thanks, worship and praise to the Father.

And we ought to pray for this reason. Someone has said, "We are a generation of people who have forgotten how to say 'Thank You.' " I feel sometimes that we are a Christian generation that has forgotten to say "Thank You" to God. Perhaps we are doing better than we did in the past. Certainly, in most places there is a greater emphasis on worship than before. Still, a lot of our praying consists of asking God for things. Little sincere thanksgiving is offered to Him. George Herbert, a 17th century British poet, said to the Lord what every believer should pray:

Thou that hast given so much to me,
Give one thing more—a grateful heart;
Not thankful when it pleaseth me,
As if Thy blessings had spare days;
But such a heart whose pulse may be
Thy praise.

Most Christians offer a prayer to God before meals. Jesus did this before He fed the 5,000, and among many present-day believers this is a firmly established practice. In fact, if we are with other Christian friends, say on a Sunday night after church for some light refreshments, we are likely to look at each other and wonder, is this enough of a meal that we ought to have prayer before we eat or not? A friend of mine was once with a minister and some other men in a public restaurant. Before they began to eat, this minister stood up and in a loud voice prayed over the food while everyone else in the place watched and listened.

I do not think such an ostentatious display of prayer is necessary, but the habit of praying before each meal is good and should be maintained. It reminds us to be thankful for God's goodness to us. It provides us with another opportunity to express gratitude to the Lord. I only wish we would always be sincere when we thus pray. I am afraid that often our prayers before meals are vain repetition. If we thank God for our food before meals, we ought really to mean it.

Jesus also prayed to ask help for Himself. One of those long night sessions of prayer Jesus spent occurred just before He chose the 12 who were to be His special disciples. The way this information is recorded in Luke suggests that Jesus prayed in order to have the Father's guidance. Jesus also prayed for power from heaven as He was about to perform certain of His miracles. He also prayed for Himself in Gethsemane.

The example of Jesus encourages us to pray for God's help and blessing upon our lives. Bob and Marie who attended a church I pastored would never express a personal request for prayer because they felt they were being selfish to do so. But we are invited by God to bring all our needs and desires to Him. We are urged to be as children coming to a loving parent. We are told that God loves to give good things to those who are His own.

Jesus also prayed for others. This is the third reason why He prayed. He prayed for Peter. He blessed little children whom He took into His arms.

He prayed for forgiveness from God for those who nailed Him to the cross. It is interesting to note from the epistles of the New Testament that Jesus continues to pray for others. We are told the now-ascended, exalted Jesus ever lives to make intercession for us.

And of course we should pray for others. A fine Christian woman began attending a church I pastored. She attended several of the mid-week prayer services and then she stopped coming. I asked her why. She said, "You sometimes divide up in groups and give everyone an opportunity to participate; and," she said, "I don't mind praying with others. But the people at your church pray for missionaries all over the world by name and you talk about specific needs. I have never learned to pray that way." We all need to learn to pray that way, for definite needs, about specific things, as we pray for others.

Finally, Jesus obviously prayed sometimes just to be in communion with His Father. Those references we already have noted of Jesus' extended periods in prayer and the record of His great prayer in John 17 reveal that Jesus often engaged in communion with the Father in heaven.

And this is a dimension of prayer we ought not to miss. Something of the blessedness of quiet communion in the presence of God is expressed by the hymn that says:

My God, is any hour so sweet,
From blush of morn to evening star
As that which calls me to Thy feet—
The hour of prayer?
No words can tell what sweet relief
There for our every want we find,
What strength for warfare, balm for grief,
What peace of mind.
Hushed is each doubt, gone every fear,
Our spirits seem in heaven to stay,
And even the penitential tear
Is wiped away.
Lord, till we reach yon blissful shore,
No privilege so dear shall be
As thus our inmost souls to pour
In prayer to Thee.

After I preached a message one Sunday on prayer, I received a letter from someone who had been a visitor in the service that day. She wrote, "I am a Lutheran missionary to Africa, presently in the United States on furlough. I was passing through your city and just dropped in to visit your church. I appreciated your message and especially your emphasis on the importance of protracted periods of communion with the Person of God in prayer." She said, "I work almost entirely alone in a difficult place. If I had not learned to draw apart and meet God in the way you talked about, I could never survive as a missionary."

Do we ever just remain quiet before Him, concentrating on His Person, thinking about Him, seeking to saturate our souls with His presence? I do not think any Christian survives very well wherever we are without this. It was a part of the prayer life of Jesus. It should be of ours.

The Bible says that God wills that we be conformed to the image of Christ. This means, in part, to pray like Jesus. And Jesus prayed often, regularly, instantly. He prayed simply, intensely extendedly. He prayed with thanksgiving, for Himself, for others and to spend time in communion with the Father. Here is a pattern we must follow.

Dr. Maurice Irvin is the editor of Alliance Life, *Colorado Springs, Colorado.*

The Lord's Prayer

CHAPTER

3

Matthew 6:9–13

by Arnold R. Fleagle

A S CONTEMPORARY DISCIPLES OF CHRIST we wrestle with the challenge of the first century followers who aimed at being like Him. In their school of learning they once approached Jesus when He was in the process of the discipline of prayer. Luke 11:1 records, "He was praying in a certain place, and when he ceased, one of his disciples said to Him, 'Lord, teach us to pray as John taught his disciples!' " Our Lord then responded with what has been labeled "The Lord's Prayer." It is found in the Sermon on the Mount in its fullest recorded form. Some scholars have labeled it "The Model Prayer" or "The Disciples' Prayer." It is a paradigm for all who would seek to pattern their prayer lives after the Prince of Prayer.

Jesus is eminently qualified to provide us a blueprint for prayer. His life was prayer personified. The four gospels mention Him praying 15 times and contain nine of His actual prayers. He seems to apply the principle of prayer in all geographical settings, at all times of the day and during His quiet moments and His crisis moments. He could pray short prayers or prevail all night in prayer. Three of His prayers were made from the cruel confines of Calvary's cross! John Wesley said that prayer was the "grand means of drawing near to God," and perhaps that was the secret of Jesus' oneness with the Father because of His constant and close communication with Him.

Jesus understood the dynamic of prayer for the 12 and for the 20th century Christian. He did not forsake us to the fog concerning prayer but left us a written pattern to copy. He recommended this pattern by saying, "Pray then like this . . . ." It was John Henry Jowett who elevated prayer above preaching by commenting, "I would rather teach one man to pray than 10 men to preach." He may have a point worth pursuing. Prayer is the main channel through which God pours His grace and gifts! Prayer is also the main channel through which we send our praises and petitions to Him!

The model prayer can be recited in less than 30 seconds and yet within its perimeters are found the primary concerns of God and man! A man studying a picture is not guaranteed he will be a painter. A man listening to music is not necessarily destined to become a musician. A man studying prayer does not insure he will become successful before God in prayer. But, by studying a masterpiece, the possibilities and proper procedures are revealed! Oh, Lord Jesus, thank you for a prayer which maps out a successful road to the throne room of the Father where we may find mercy and grace to help in time of need!

Greeting God

Jesus made a revolutionary change in the greeting which He prescribed for the model prayer. His approach to God begins with the words, "Our Father." Prior to this teaching no saint had called God "Father." This was a theological watershed in prayer. In terms of Jewish usage in the Old Testament the term "father" was employed collectively but not intimately, and God was not conceptualized in a familiar and filial sense. God is now to be addressed as a child addresses the father in his family. Both Jesus and Paul used the word "Abba" to speak to God in prayer and this is even more astonishing, for the most precise translation of Abba is "Daddy." That may sound unusual and too elementary for our sophisticated taste, but Jesus' inference is clear. We are to pray to God with the simple trust, innocence and confidence of a child who comes to his father who is the source of his provision and protection. I cannot imagine my sons, Matthew and Marc, seeking me out for conversation and saying to me,

"I have come to speak to you, The Right Most Reverend Arnold R. Fleagle." That would be unnatural and awkward. Yet, our prayer lives are often starchy and stiff as we reach out to God with Victorian propriety rather than childlike dependency!

The greeting of our God as a father in prayer has overwhelming recommendation in the life of Jesus Himself. In *eight* of the *nine* recorded prayers of Jesus Christ, He greets God with the description Father. His prayer from the cross provides the only exception when He quotes David's words in Psalm 22:1 (KJV), "My God, My God, why hast thou forsaken me." Except for this quotation He enters in conversation with the greeting befitting a child, "Father." The Prince's prayer pattern commences with a family flavor and it should be the trademark of our prayer lives to follow the Master plan of prayer. "Heavenly Father" or "Father in Heaven" is the proper protocol for most participants of prayer. There are exceptions in Scripture such as Stephen praying to the Lord Jesus when he was being stoned to death, but the prevailing prelude to our praises and petitions is to be the acknowledgement of God as our Father.

Jesus planted balance into the soil of this greeting. "Our Father" speaks of immanence, but "in heaven" speaks of transcendence! Yes, He is Father, but *He* is not to be thought of flippantly, irreverently or as "my buddy." "In heaven" speaks of the otherness of

God, the sovereignty of God, the special nature of this Heavenly Father. The concept of God has been trivialized in the 20th century. Jesus insured that we would approach God in personal terms, but also qualified His fatherly role with a reference to somewhere beyond our experience and comprehension.

God's Concerns

The Prince's prayer pattern was to commence with God's concerns. As in the Ten Commandments where the first four commandments are focused upon God and the remaining six focused upon man, so the model prayer first addresses three concerns of God before it advances to three concerns of man. Prayer should first address God's priorities. So often we pray in the hurry and heat of crisis, and there is little thought of God—just the panic and pressure of our own dilemma. Jesus began with God and if one wants to be successful, he will open prayer at the Divine doorstep!

"Hallowed be your name" is the first concern of God. The Word, worship and the world have been designed for God's glory. The word hallowed—the Greek word is *hagiazo*—means to set apart. This word is used for "sanctify" in the New Testament and lends a special and holy significance to anything or anyone it describes. In prayer there should be a reverence of God's name and character, a humbling of ourselves before the great "I AM!" When you address the Father in prayer, respect His character, recognize His authority!

"Your kingdom come" is the concern of God as He takes reign over our hearts and ultimately over all earth and heaven. The kingdom is a dynamic concept, one which encompasses the past, present and future. The believer must understand the kingdom as now, but not yet. The kingdom is here in us, but its final consummation is still to be awaited. The kingdom is present in its embryonic stages, but the eschatological kingdom is not yet established until Jesus institutes His Messianic reign. The Prince of this world still possesses great and frightening power, but his time is short and his defeat will be final forever. This aspect of prayer reminds the child that he is in enemy territory, that he is an alien in this land, that he is a part of a larger plan and purpose, the kingdom of God.

"Your will be done" was a primary petition of Jesus because God's will is preeminent in the sphere of men. He prayed that the Father's will would supercede His will. This is sometimes an easy prayer, but when we reach Gethsemane's Garden it becomes very difficult to articulate. God's will is sometimes painful, sometimes pleasant, but always perfect! This is critical to the life of the Christian. Our wills must be swallowed up in God's will. This is a major concern of the Father and is a salient section of the believer's prayer life. If we mean it, God will honor us and we will invest in the greatest of all strategies, His divine will. If we don't pray for His will we will face the ultimate opponent, God Himself. Jonah, the Bible says, was told the will of God; then the Scriptures say, "But Jonah." That contrary conjunction indicates we are acting contradictorily. Then the Scriptures say, "But God." Don't butt up against God or you may face the rebuttal of your life.

The focus on God's concerns is an expression of praise to His person and work in our world. "Your name," "your kingdom," "your will" give God first place, and that is the only place He is satisfied with for He stands above and beyond all other creatures. Throughout Isaiah we read, "I am the Lord, beside me there is no other!" Elevating God, magnifying God, praising God, that is the Prince's prayer pattern. Jesus called Him, "Lord of heaven and earth" (Luke 10:21).

Man's Concerns

Subsequent to praying for God's concerns it is our privilege to pray for our own personal concerns. Jesus begins the recital of human need with a request for daily bread. There is nothing spiritually wrong with making petition for provision. In creation, God provided that Adam and Eve could freely eat of every tree of the garden except one (Genesis 2:16). The Lord fed the multitudes at least two different times. In the New Testament church there was not a "needy person" among them. To refuse to pray for these needs leads to sinful pride and independence from God. Andrew Murray in his famous classic, *With Christ in the School of Prayer,* outlined our natural expectancy by writing, "A master cares for the food of his servant, a general of his soldiers, a father for his child" (p. 30). Daily bread is a function of the Father in behalf of His children.

"Forgive us our debts [sins]" is a crucial component of the model prayer. Jesus is placing at the center of man's concerns the purification of his heart. If everyone sincerely and genuinely prayed the model prayer by faith, all would be gloriously forgiven and saved. It is God's highest pleasure to heal our hearts of spiritual cancer! Heaven is elated at the coming home of the prodigal son to renewed sonship! This prayer encompasses the forgiveness of the child of God, who may be positionally in Christ, but whose life manifests blemishes and spots. Corrie Ten Boom taught that God casts our sins into the deepest sea, and then puts up a sign which reads, "No Fishing Allowed." Jesus realized the frailty of our wills and natures and provided a remedy in the model prayer. However, one word of caution: the prayer includes the qualifier, *as we also have forgiven our debtors,* which was labeled the "terrible petition" by the early church father, Augustine. God expects us to act in like manner as

He has acted on our behalf. It was General James Ogelthorpe who said to John Wesley, "I will never forgive." "Then I hope, sir," replied Wesley, "you never sin." A stoic, stubborn attitude toward one who has wronged us is like placing a piece of sheet metal over a crimson rose so it cannot receive the rain. Amos and Andy, a comedy duo from a couple of generations ago, still has contemporary value. There was a big man who would slap Andy across the chest whenever they met. Andy finally had his quota of this abuse and told Amos, "I am fixed for him. I put a stick of dynamite in my vest pocket and the next time he slaps me he is going to get his hand blown off."

Those who are forgiven are to be forgiving people! This is a theme of proper prayer.

"Lead us not into temptation, but deliver us from the evil one" is the final concern of man in this three-fold petition. Jesus in His High Priestly prayer highlighted the concern again, "My prayer is not that you take them out of the world but that you protect them from the evil one" (John 17:15). We cannot afford the mentality of the lady who stood up in midweek prayer meeting and declared, "I'm so glad the devil doesn't tempt me any more." That is an unhealthy and ill-advised testimony. George Duncan stated, "The more you mean to God the more you mean to the devil." Even the Messiah was tempted by the prince of this world. We are in danger, and we sometimes are deficient, but we can be delivered! "To him who is able to keep you from falling and to present you before his glorious presence . . ." is Jude's assessment of the Father's care over His kin (Jude 24). "No temptation has seized you except what is common to man. And God is faithful; he will not let you be tempted beyond what you can bear. But when you are tempted, he will also provide a way out so that you can stand up under it" (1 Corinthians 10:13) was the encouragement of Paul to the Corinthians.

It is accurate to state that temptations, tests and trials are a given for the followers of Jesus Christ. They will serve as stumbling blocks or stepping stones. The Old Testament offers Joseph and Esther as overcomers and Cain and Lot's wife as overcome! The New Testament presents Peter as ample evidence that a believer can go both ways in his or her spiritual journey. We are not to assume deliverance but we are to pray specifically for it!

Doxology

Many versions record that Jesus comes full circle in the model prayer by closing it with a word of praise, a doxology to God! "For thine is the kingdom, the power, the glory" (KJV) is a three-fold trumpet heralding the Father for His Person and Work! This addendum serves as an exclamation point to this pattern prayer. It accentuates the reign of God, His ability to sustain that regency and the glory which is due Him because of His kingship in history and beyond it!

Conclusion

The model prayer provides a master blueprint for the Christians of all ages and in all ages to be in living relationship with the great Parent of all peoples! Many have discounted prayer; *our Lord practiced it and promoted it!* Dennis Kinlaw remarked, following the Asbury Revival of 1970, "Give me one divine moment when God acts and I say that moment is far superior to all the human efforts of man throughout the centuries." Prayer is the key which opens the door to many of these moments.

In his discussion of the supernatural in *Present Truths*, A.B. Simpson declares:

There is no wonder more supernatural and divine in the life of the believer than the mystery and the ministry of prayer. . . . Wonder of wonders! Mystery of mysteries! Miracle of miracles! The hand of the child touching the arm of the Father and moving the wheels of the universe.

Beloved, this is your supernatural place and mine, and over its gates we read the inspiring invitation, "Thus saith the Lord . . . Call unto me, and I will answer thee, and shew thee great and mighty things, which thou knowest not" (pp. 43–44).

Dr. Arnold R. Fleagle is the Senior Pastor of Immanuel Alliance Church, Mechanicsburg, Pennsylvania.

	Prayer Is More
CHAPTER	**than Asking**
4	*by Bill J. Vaughn*

Prayer Is More than Asking

CHAPTER 4

by Bill J. Vaughn

W E LIVE IN A WORLD that has as its theme song, "Buy now, pay later," and I'm not sure but maybe this attitude has carried over into our prayer lives. I do right now what I want, and then I pray that God will bless it and make it good.

In James 4:3–6 we read these familiar verses:

> When you ask, you do not receive, because you ask with wrong motives, that you may spend what you get on your passions. You adulterous people, don't you know that friendship with the world is hatred toward God? Anyone who chooses to be a friend of the world becomes an enemy of God. Or do you think Scripture says without reason that the spirit he caused to live in us tends toward envy, but he gives us more grace? That is why Scripture says: "God opposes the proud but gives grace to the humble."

Prayer is not just a good idea. It is *all important* and it is for everyone. We are communicating with our all powerful Lord. In my early years as a Christian I struggled with prayer. I was aware that it was an important part of the Christian life but I didn't ask many questions about it because, honestly, I didn't enjoy it very much. In fact, I remember as a teenager from a non-Christian home attending Wednesday night prayer meeting. I found myself bored and even confused. Can you believe that?

My Wrong Motives

I had to force myself to pray. It was something that I had to do. That is really bad, but it actually gets worse, because other times I did it for a "reward"—you know, "God, do this or do that." If my communication with my friends and family had been as difficult and selfish as my communication with God, I would have been a very lonely teenager. If I had to force myself to spend time with a friend, finding myself bored and my mind straying, I seriously doubt that the friendship would survive. You don't find yourself bored with a friend. You don't find yourself watching the clock on the wall. No, you enjoy your friend and time seems to fly when you are with him or her. You don't say to your friend, "I'll spend time with you *if* you reward me for it." Or, "I'll spend time with you *if* you do what I ask."

How could our Lord who loves us so much be pleased with that kind of an attitude? How could God be pleased with that kind of praying? God could not have been pleased with me—I wasn't even pleased with myself. You see, we don't pray because we're forced to—that's just dead works. God is not going to be happy with our deals—you know, "I'll do this *if* You do that. I will follow You *if* You will take me where I want to go. I will do Your will *if* if matches my will."

Love Should Move Us to Pray

God wants our love. Our motivation as individuals and as a church has to be love. And, our love has to be willingly and joyfully given. The verse informing us that God loves a cheerful giver can be applied more broadly than just to money. Prayer should be one of the greatest pleasures in life.

It certainly has to be the greatest gift to mankind. We simply call on God the Creator of heaven and earth at any time, any place and in any situation or set of circumstances. What a tremendous, amazing, wonderful gift! We should not only use that gift, but we should improve and cultivate it.

James says, "When you ask, you do not receive, because you ask with wrong motives that you may spend what you get on your own pleasures."

Is it possible that equating "asking" with "prayer"

is part of our problem? If prayer is conversation with a friend, then it has to involve more than needs and requests. Before you ask God for something, think about what He has already given to you. Why should God give more if you are not using what He has already given you?

Already Generous

I heard once about a father who gave his son $500 for his graduation trip. And, being the good father he was, he said to his son, "If you have an emergency and your money runs out, give me a call." About three hours later his son called and asked his dad if he could send another $100. The father was more than a little shocked.

"Where is the $500 that I gave you? What did you do with it?"

"Well, I . . . I . . . haven't used it yet," the son answered.

"Then why are you asking me for $100 more? When you spend the $500 I gave you, let me know, and maybe I will give you more."

God has already been generous to us. One of the greatest things He has given us is a mind, and He expects us to use it. Sometimes we don't want to use our minds and we say things like, "Lord, help me pass this test," or "Lord, help me to not run out of gas," or "Lord, help me to be able to pay all our bills."

I know there may be exceptions, but please realize they are exceptions. I believe God would say, "Use your head. If you want to pass your test, study, or you will fail. Don't put this on Me. If you don't want to run out of gas, use your head and buy more before you run out." This is our problem, not a prayer problem. If we cannot pay our bills because more is going out than is coming in, I believe God would say we should use our heads—either make more money or spend less. There are actually many Christians who feel God has failed them because He didn't do what they asked Him to do—like help them pass the test or pay the bills.

Often we find ourselves pleading with God for something He has already given us. Let's reflect on the abundance of things that God has already given to us. The son with the graduation money doesn't see the $500 gift as a miracle; he is thinking that more would represent a miracle.

We Need to Use Our Heads

Actually, a great resource for many of our prayers is our heads. If someone is cold and hungry, we don't have to pray that he will be warm and well fed—we need to give him clothing and food. An appropriate prayer could be, "Lord, open the door for me to share with these people in need. Show them through me that You love them." Sometimes we do not see answers simply because we ask the wrong things.

I do not know what percentage of Christians is addicted to worry. But I do believe they can drive the calmest of people to biting their nails. Our psychological as well as our physical needs are important to God and He instructs us to be anxious for nothing. When we face difficult times God has promised to give us peace. All too often, we don't really see our prayers answered because we are praying about things that really don't call for prayer and failing to seek God's guidance in matters that only He knows about.

Leave It with Jesus

Do you remember the first of Jesus' miracles? The great wedding was taking place, and they ran out of wine. Mary, the mother of Jesus, was the one who noticed, and she called to her son, "Jesus, we do not have any more wine." She didn't say, "Son, make wine." She didn't tell Jesus what to do—she simply brought the problem to Him. If we had only been there to tell Mary to tell Jesus to make more wine and that it was needed now, more than likely the second miracle would have been the first. But Mary simply said to her son, "They have no more wine." This should teach us something about casting all our anxieties upon Him because He cares. Jesus tells us to just further His kingdom and all these things will be given to us.

We spend too much of our prayer time asking. Do you ever wonder why it is so difficult to get the things we pray for? *It is because we are not seeking first the kingdom.* If we were seeking first the kingdom, we would have the other things without having to ask for them.

What does it mean to seek the kingdom? It means for us to make sure that God's will has become our will. Another way to say it is to make sure that it has become our will to do His will.

Praying Continually

There is no doubt about it. Prayer (meaning communication with our Lord) should become natural, important and enjoyable. When we pray, we should reflect in our prayer time how to use the tremendous resources and miracles that God has already given to us.

As I was growing up it seemed to me that the idea of praying without ceasing was interpreted by some as praying super-long prayers. It was almost like turning in our *prayer time* in order to determine for how much blessing we should be compensated. If we examine the Scriptures, we discover that the greatest prayers are really very short.

Some of us grew up hearing people shout in their prayers. The Scriptures do not say anywhere "according to your lungs," or "according to your time." They say, "according to your faith." Please don't misunderstand; we are to pray constantly and about all things, but our prayers should always be seeking first the kingdom of God.

God's Will First

It would appear that part of our prayer effort should be to find God's will and get His direction. Our prayer life should be carefully focused on God's will, on what God wants. Our will should be to seek His will.

Elijah walked up to his rebuilt altar and prayed:

> O LORD, God of Abraham, Isaac and Israel, let it be known today that you are God in Israel and that I am your servant and have done all these things at your command. Answer me, O LORD, answer me, so these people will know that you, O LORD, are God, and that you are turning their hearts back again. (1 Kings 18:36–37)

Prayer Is Communion

Our God is God. He is intelligent, and He is always there. He knows our need before we even ask. We are to pray without ceasing, but that does not mean we are to ask without ceasing. It also includes fellowship and friendship. Our communication should become natural and easy—not strained and strange. It's not a matter of repeating; it's a matter of cultivating our relationship with God.

Jesus wants to make me a better spouse and parent and grandparent, pastor, friend and citizen. He wants my light to shine brighter and my salt to be saltier. He wants me to further His kingdom and seek it first. He wants the same for you.

I end with a comment and a prayer by A.W. Tozer:

You and I are in little (our sins excepted) what God is in large. Being made in His image we have within us the capacity to know Him. In our sins we lack only the power. The moment the Spirit has quickened us to life in regeneration our whole being senses its kinship to God and leaps up in joyous recognition. That is the heavenly birth without which we cannot see the Kingdom of God. It is, however, not an end but an inception, for now begins the glorious pursuit, the heart's happy exploration of the infinite riches of the Godhead. That is where we begin, I say, but where we stop no man has yet discovered, for there is in the awful and mysterious depths of the Triune God neither limit nor end. (*The Best of A.W. Tozer,* p. 15)

O God, I have tasted Thy goodness, and it has both satisfied me and made me thirsty for more. I am painfully conscious of my need of further grace. I am ashamed of my lack of desire. O

God, the Triune God, I want to want Thee; I long to be filled with longing; I thirst to be made more thirsty still. Show me Thy glory, I pray Thee, that so I may know Thee indeed. Begin in mercy a new work of love within me. Say to my soul, "Rise up, my love, my fair one, and come away." Then give me grace to rise and follow Thee up from this misty lowland where I have wandered so long. In Jesus' Name, Amen. (p. 19)

Rev. Bill J. Vaughn is the superintendent of the South Pacific District in Rancho Cucamonga, California.

Pray for Israel

by Abraham Sandler

SOME YEARS AGO A TEENAGE Jewish boy wound up in a Bible study conducted in Philadelphia by a Christian and Missionary Alliance missionary. The boy had but one reason for being there: he wanted to play on the group's ball team, and it was open only to those who attended the Bible study.

Nothing else could have persuaded this boy to join a Bible study sponsored by Christians. He was bitter against Christians because they had persecuted his people. More than once he himself had been the target of anti-Semitism.

In the Bible study he was less than a model student. During the discussions he cut up and fooled around and generally kept the meeting in disarray. In exasperation the leader put it on the line: "Either you be quiet, or you can't stay!" And when he refused to behave, the leader kept his word. Even as the boy was being expelled he was defiant: "I'm *never* coming back to this place again!"

But he did go back—the next week. At the time

he was not aware that the leader had sent a letter to hundreds of praying people, asking them to pray that a certain 15-year-old boy would return, would behave and would be saved. He returned, he behaved and, four weeks later, he received Messiah-Jesus into his life.

The details of that story are familiar to me, for I was the 15-year-old boy.

Pray for Jerusalem

"Every time a Christian picks up his Bible," wrote A.W. Tozer, "he is reminded of his debt to the Jewish people. It is an astonishing thing that multitudes of Bible students and lovers of the truth should calmly overlook their obligation to Israel (Romans 1:16).

"Pray for the peace of Jerusalem" is more than a cliché. It is a scriptural command (Psalm 122:6) given by God to all His people. Hear as Jesus looked at Jerusalem from the Mount of Olives and wept as he cried out, "O Jerusalem, Jerusalem, you who kill the prophets and stone those sent to you, how often I have longed to gather your children together, as a hen gathers her chicks under her wings, but you were not willing!" (Luke 13:34).

Are you obeying God's command to pray for the peace of Jerusalem? Are you praying for God's specially chosen people?

Your Prayers Are Not Unanswered

Jodi was a young Jewish woman in her early 20s when she prayed to receive Jesus as her Messiah-Savior. Her older sister, Arlene, insisted she was crazy. Moreover, Arlene considered all the people at our Bible study crazy. *She* would never attend a Bible study!

We began to pray for Arlene. Finally word reached us that Arlene planned to visit our study. But—and she made this very clear—she didn't want to talk to me. Sure enough, Arlene came to the Bible study she said she would never attend. And she talked with *me* for 45 minutes. Three days later, Arlene was "crazy" too.

Arlene's parents and grandmother were angry. Now two of the family had put their faith in Jesus-Messiah. They forbade Arlene and Jodi to speak about either Abe Sandler or Jesus in their house. (That put me in pretty good company, I thought!)

More to the Story

The story does not end there. A short time later Arlene had occasion to come to me for some counsel. When she reported to her grandmother what I had said, the grandmother told her it was good advice and urged her to follow it. About a week later my phone rang. It was Arlene's grandmother.

"Mr. Sandler," she said, "I also have a problem. Maybe you could give me some advice." She went on to describe a family rift between a niece and her. Prayerfully, I suggested a possible course of action.

"Oh, that won't work," the grandmother insisted. "My niece is as stubborn as a mule!"

"Then all I can do is pray she will have a change of heart."

"You can pray," the grandmother allowed, "but it won't work. My niece is as stubborn as a mule."

A few days later as Arlene entered our Bible study, she was bursting with excitement. "You'll never guess what happened," she began. "My grandmother's niece phoned her and said, 'I've had a change of heart!'"

Guess who baked me a birthday cake that year! You're right. It was Arlene's grandmother. I began visiting the home and had the privilege of leading the mother to faith in Jesus.

Pray for Israel and Be Blessed

J. Hudson Taylor, the famous missionary to China, on January 1 of each year used to mail a gift of money to a London-based Jewish missionary. On the bottom of the check he would write "Romans 1:16—to the Jew first." After receiving Taylor's letter and gift, the missionary would respond with a thank-you note, enclosing a contribution for Hudson Taylor's work in China. On the bottom of his check he would write, "Romans 1:16—and also to the Gentile."

That exchange makes a point that the Scriptures also make. The full text of Psalm 122:6 reads this way: "Pray for the peace of Jerusalem: / 'May those who love you be secure.' " In Hebrew an interesting and beautiful wordplay binds together *pray, peace, Jerusalem* and *secure. Peace* connotes both security and prosperity. God's blessing attends those who have at heart the welfare of Jerusalem and its people.

A Testimony of Blessing

I was in Mars, Pennsylvania, where I had been invited for a Sunday ministry. As Pastor Paul Cope introduced me to his large congregation, he shared this story: His first pastorate had been a small charge. The church struggled to pay its monthly bills. One Sunday morning a retired minister spoke, taking as his text Genesis 12:1-3, God's covenant-promise to Abraham. Picking up on God's promise to "bless those who bless [Israel]," the minister assured his listeners that God would bless them if they prayed faithfully for Israel and gave toward the evangelization of Jewish people.

The church's board later discussed the message and determined to set aside one Wednesday night prayer meeting each month to pray specifically for Jewish evangelism. The offering that night would be put to the same cause. Within a month after initiating this new course, the church was able for the first time to pay its bills on time. And God continued to prosper the church.

When Pastor Cope was invited to be minister of the Alliance church in Mars, his one stipulation was that they initiate the same Wednesday evening procedure. The church agreed—with great subsequent blessing. Just a year before, it had given a group of members to begin a daughter church, and already it had welcomed more new people than it had sent forth. Sunday attendance was running more than 400.

God assured Abraham, "I will bless those who bless you."

Pray for Israel's Future

It is significant that from Jerusalem's destruction in A.D. 70 until the middle of this century, no major prophecy concerning Israel and its land was fulfilled—a period of almost 1,900 years. Jesus Himself, referring to His Jewish kinspeople, said, "They will fall by the sword and will be taken as prisoners to all the nations. Jerusalem will be trampled on by the Gentiles until the times of the Gentiles are fulfilled" (Luke 21:24).

Then on May 14, 1948, God began to regather His people. On that date Israel became an independent nation for the first time in more than 2,500 years. And in June, 1967, during the "Six-Day War," Israel recovered all of Jerusalem. I recall the very place I was standing in a Philadelphia supermarket when news came over the radio that Israeli soldiers had taken Jerusalem. Tears streamed down my face as I realized (1) the holiest place in all the world to Jewish hearts was now back in our hands and (2) the prophecy of Jesus Christ had just been fulfilled.

A New Openness

I can testify that from that point on we have seen a new openness among Jewish people toward the gospel. Tens of thousands worldwide have received Jesus as their Messiah-Savior.

Phyllis was 19 when she first came to our Bible study. On her second visit she asked if she could say something to the group before the study began. I gave permission.

"Last night," Phyllis announced, "I prayed to receive Jesus as my Messiah!" Pandemonium broke out in the room. Everyone began to hug and kiss her. A fellow sitting in my rocking chair shouted "Hallelujah!" and threw up his arms with such force that the chair fell apart, landing him on the floor.

Phyllis began to grow in the Lord. Three months later, her parents decided to get her "straightened out," so they took her to a rabbi. The rabbi opined that she was (1) looking for something, (2) rebellious, or else (3) deranged "upstairs." The parents, seizing on the last-mentioned, decided to try a psychiatrist.

Phyllis was upset about the prospects of visiting a psychiatrist, so she talked to my wife, Janet, about it. Janet opened the Scriptures to Matthew 10:18-20 and read Jesus' words: " 'On my account you will be brought before governors and kings as witnesses to them and to the Gentiles. But when they arrest you, do not worry about what to say or how to say it. At that time you will be given what to say, for it will not be you speaking, but the Spirit of your Father speaking through you.' "

A Nervous Psychiatrist

Jesus did not mention psychiatrists specifically, but Phyllis understood that she had nothing to worry about. So she went for her appointment.

"Why are you here?" the psychiatrist wanted to know.

"My parents asked me to see you."

"Your parents? You don't have to do what your parents say!"

"Yes, I do."

"No, you don't!"

"Yes, I do."

"Why do you keep on saying that?"

"Because the Bible says to honor and obey your parents."

"The Bible? You believe the Bible?"

"Yes!"

The doctor began asking this "baby" questions about the Bible. God gave Phyllis appropriate answers. Every time she answered a question, the psychiatrist got more nervous. By the end of the interview, *he* was the one in need of an analyst!

Sam, Florence and Beyond

I went to see Sam and his wife, Florence, at their home. Together we looked at the Scriptures, examining the Messianic prophecies. I explained how Yeshua-Jesus had fulfilled them. That very afternoon they prayed the penitent's prayer. Three days later they showed up at Messiah's Lighthouse, the Alliance Jewish congregation in Philadelphia. Suddenly, right in the middle of the service, Sam stood to his feet and said, "I just want everyone here to know that three days ago I found out that Jesus was my Jewish Messiah and He saved me."

Sam wanted me to talk with his father. Sam's dad was one of the elders of the synagogue I attended as a boy, and I was a little nervous. But Sam and I prayed together and then we went to see him. For 30 minutes I opened the Scriptures and shared the Messianic prophecies of the Old Testament. And that 82-year-old Orthodox Jewish man prayed to receive Jesus as his Messiah. It was one of the great thrills of my life.

A Personal Testimony

I was raised in a religious Jewish home. When I declared to my family my faith in Jesus, I was threatened with a funeral. For many years my family treated me with disdain. One of my brothers said he would blow my brains out with his shotgun if I didn't stop talking to him about Jesus.

My only resource was God, and my only weapon was prayer. Over the years, in answer to prayer, first my father came to faith in Christ. That was five years after my salvation. Almost 25 years later, Mother received Jesus as her Messiah. Jack, my brother who threatened me with his shotgun, more recently told me, "You can talk to me about Jesus anytime you want to. I can see that you and your family have something. But I'm not quite ready to receive Him yet. Maybe God has to hit me over the head to make me see it." Will you please pray with me for Jack, that God will bring him to faith?

My oldest brother, a successful musician, always responded to my witness with "I'm glad for what it has done for you, but I don't need it." Then one day I got a phone call from Laura, his wife, saying that Herman had brain cancer. Doctors gave him six months. I went to see him. We had a good visit, but his response to my witness was still the same. I continued to pray for Herman's salvation. Others joined me in petitioning heaven.

Another Phone Call

Some months later, another call came from Laura. Doctors were now saying three weeks. "But don't try to come out," Laura advised. "Herman is not able to hold a conversation. He might not even recognize you."

I felt strongly that I should go, so I flew to California. Laura picked me up at the airport, and we drove directly to the house. When I walked into my brother's room he looked at me and said, "Abe, it's so good to see you! I'm glad you came." Laura was dumbfounded.

I was with Herman for two days. The night before I left I was sitting alone with him in his room. I prayed inwardly, asking God what to do. For 29 years I had witnessed to this man, and he had rejected my witness every time.

"Abe," my brother began without my saying anything, "ever since you were here the first time, I have been thinking about Jesus. I would like to make Him a part of my life." This time, *I* was dumbfounded!

"Do you really believe that Jesus is your Messiah?" I finally asked.

"Yes!"

"And do you realize you are a sinner and only Jesus' blood can cleanse you?"

Again, "Yes!"

We prayed together, he following me in a prayer

of repentance and trust in Jesus the Messiah-Savior.

"Abe," he said when we had finished, "I feel great. We've got to tell my wife about this!"

I left the next day. Three weeks later Herman died. But I know he is with the Lord. I will see him again because he trusted in Jesus.

Conclusion

Those are a few of the trophies of God's grace. But 16 million of my people have not yet understood the good news that Yeshua-Jesus is their Messiah and Redeemer. Worse, they will not understand unless you and millions of other Christians make a regular commitment to "pray for the peace of Jerusalem."

Will you do it?

Rev. Abe Sandler is an Alliance evangelist and church planter among Jewish people in the United States. He resides in Philadelphia, Pennsylvania.

CHAPTER	Prayer and
6	Missions

by Julie R. Fehr

MISSIONARY ANITA READER AND I, together with five Tsogo workers, were on a two-week evangelistic trip in a restricted-entry gold-mining zone in Gabon. We were where roads end and isolation begins—an isolation imposed by the jungle and the Ministry of Mines.

The Dibua people to whom we had come to minister had never before heard a clear presentation of who God is. Yet they were ready to respond. At this very first preaching of the gospel, God was intervening in their lives through salvation, healings and other phenomena.

One afternoon during the campaign, we were relaxing in a Dibua village where time and history seemed to stand still. I was reading an eight-month-old issue of what was then *The Alliance Witness*. It had arrived at my house just before we left for our ministry trip. There on the page of late-breaking missionary prayer requests was information about our proposed evangelistic effort to the unreached Dibua! Circumstances beyond our control had delayed our trip. How strange it felt to read that "old" prayer request while I was at the scene of the answers! I translated the paragraph for the team members.

"That's it!" exclaimed Pastor Joel. "That's it! That is why we are seeing such unbelievable results on this first trip to these totally unevangelized Dibua people! While we were delayed and praying in our villages, the readers of that magazine, wherever it is mailed around the world, were also praying. The work was already being done before we even got here. All around the world, Alliance people were interceding before God as a result of that prayer request. We are not isolated from the rest of God's people!"

"We All Lift Our Arms before the Same God!"

An awesome silence tied us together in that remote hut. Then Okaba, an elder with the gift of evangelism, said softly, "The church! That's the church from around the world. We all lift our arms before the same God!" The moment and the room seemed to be peopled with a multi-national gathering of praying saints.

Pastor Joel picked up the conversation again. He explained how he had seen a rotating world globe that helped him understand the time zones. "While we sleep others are awake and vice versa. There is always someone praying somewhere. From around the world, night and day, we are before the Father."

As one or two raindrops striking jungle foliage signal the arrival of a storm, so those insightful remarks led to an outpouring of praise as one, then another of our team thanked God for His marvelous worldwide network, the body of praying believers, deluging the throne night and day. We thanked God for our incredible privilege as evangelists to witness the answers to prayer in the Dibua area while many others who had served the Lord faithfully in prayer would have to settle for only hearing news of what God was doing.

In that hallowed moment we became aware that prayer and praise at the Father's throne served as a powerful bond to tie together the churches of distant continents. Although most of those who were praying would never meet on earth, we were bound to each other by the Holy Spirit, in Christ, before the Father.

Prayer is Supra-Cultural

Prayer is cross-cultural and multi-cultural in practice and in results. It is supra-cultural as, far above and beyond all culture, each believer in his or her place in the heavenlies is with Christ exercising spiritual authority. Prayer is the ultimate in missionary action.

If the ground at the foot of the cross is level for all to come to salvation by the same Way, then that throne room in the heavenlies where we believers exercise our prayer rights as God's children is also level. All who are in Christ are to pray for each other.

We want to look at prayer as it relates to missions by examining a framework of selected biblical expressions.

"We Wrestle Not Against Flesh and Blood . . ." (Ephesians 6:12)

The words "spiritual warfare" mean that there are intangible and spiritual foes. They also imply that those who will do victorious battle will be continually filled with God's Spirit (Ephesians 5:18). The language of God in His Word is filled with warfare terminology. It commands us to draw nigh to God and then "resist" the enemy and he will flee from us (James 4:7–8). Jesus explained His warfare plan in terms of binding the strongman and casting out devils by the Spirit of God (Matthew 12:29). The Word speaks of pulling down strongholds, of casting down imaginations which exalt themselves against the knowledge of God and bringing our thoughts into captivity to Christ (2 Corinthians 10:5).

The Lord allowed some major problems and spirit-world confrontations to hit His Church among the Tsogo so that together we would learn to wrestle in prayer against the enemy. They excessively attributed everything to him. I, as a student of anthropology, excessively attributed everything to Tsogo superstition. Truth lay somewhere between us, in the Word. The Tsogo believers taught me to take God at His word and resist the enemy in prayer, bind the strongman, cast down strongholds and claim victory from our position of authority in the heavenlies. Together we learned to focus on the deeper life and walk in the fullness of the Holy Spirit.

I watched a Tsogo mother denounce the enemy's attack on her child when it awoke screaming from bad dreams at night. I sat with young couples as they prayed a hedge of protection about their homes, setting them apart for God in a village filled with traditional cultic practices. I sat with deaconesses and deacons as they tested the spirit speaking in an unknown tongue and discovered it was not the Holy Spirit. We were learning together. This too was our fellowship in the gospel. It was unlike the "warm fuzzy" feeling often referred to as fellowship. It was dynamic, warm partnership of battle.

The church among the Tsogo people prayed for the salvation of my younger brother and bound the spirit of blindness that prevented him from seeing the truth of the gospel. As they perceived it, he lived in a country and a home flooded with gospel influence; therefore, his spiritual blindness was deliberate. Prayer had to also be deliberate. They persevered as did the rest of my family. Within a year my brother made a lasting commitment to God.

Warfare praying for God's servants around the world means claiming for God those areas of a missionary's and pastor's mind which they have not yet allowed the Holy Spirit to renew through the Word. This includes all areas of moral purity. Few mission fields have not experienced the trauma of moral failure on the part of its spiritual leadership.

Battling for the minds of mission and church leadership also includes dealing with attitudes of superiority, paternalism and subtle racism where the enemy retains strongholds.

We may justify these attitudes by saying, "The nationals are not ready." This can be a valid statement and yet our personal testimonies, sincerely given, attest to the fact that we too were not particularly ready when God entrusted to us the work of the ministry. The Holy Spirit, given free course, gives discernment to know those who are "capable" or "apt" to assume ministry within the church (1 Timothy 3:2; 2 Timothy 2:24). "Brethren, pray for us" (1 Thessalonians 5:25).

"Wrestling" is not passive praying. From our position in the heavenlies the Church of Jesus Christ spans oceans and continents in common combat for the glory of her King. In warfare prayer the Church appropriates what Christ has already acquired for us.

"Pray for Each Other" (James 5:16)

James urges believers to pray for each other in the context of physical sickness. Nonetheless, the apostle Paul repeatedly assured the first century churches that he was praying for them, and he urged the believers to pray as well for their messenger. "Pray for us that the message of the Lord may spread rapidly and be honored," Paul exhorted the Thessalonian Christians (2 Thessalonians 3:1). His implication is that the receiving church in Thessalonica was expected to pray for other receiving churches.

Bibili, a young Gabonese dental technician and TEE (Theological Education by Extension) student, asked me one day, "These TEE textbooks we use— who writes them? Who are these teachers who lead us step by step through the Bible?" I pointed out the authors' names on the cover.

"No," Bibili insisted. "Who *are* they? What kind of struggles must they go through to give us these spiritual insights? How do they schedule their time so they can do this writing? Who prays for them? Why don't we pray for them in our classes?"

Why not indeed! To me they were names on our Theological Education by Extension textbooks. Bibili saw them as partners with her in ministry, joint heirs with Christ at the throne. She prayed for them. She motivated others to pray for them.

"Mentioning You in Our Prayers"
(1 Thessalonians 1:2)

Paul, as we noted also above, though absent from the receiving church, assured them of his prayers. We can effectively pray for our missionaries when we pray for the receiving church—the national believers. Frequently that which exhausts, discourages or otherwise brings stress and distress to a missionary is the strain of leading men and women into maturity in Christ. Pagan systems are powerful. Family pressures can be intense. Living pure, godly lives in such a setting is not easy.

Rather than merely praying for the missionary to be in good health and to be encouraged, your prayers can better focus on the real issues. Intercede for the spiritual maturation of those with whom the missionary works, those whom he or she ministers to. Most missionaries have family members and prayer partners who remember them regularly. National Christians may have no such support, yet they contend against forces bent on drawing them back into the pagan context. Who, then, will pray for the national believers?

"If We Ask Anything According to His Will, He Hears Us" (1 John 5:14).

What is God's will in the worldwide mission He has given to His church? A Gabonese colleague of mine explained the above Scripture by saying: "We should stick to God's 'want' list." Then he quoted: "God . . . wants all men to be saved and to come to a knowledge of the truth" (1 Timothy 2:4). "The Lord is . . . not wanting anyone to perish, but everyone to come to repentance" (2 Peter 3:9). My friend was right. The primary reason for missions and for praying for missions is to bring men and women to salvation. Praying in God's will means keeping as our ultimate goal the salvation of people everywhere and bringing them into fellowship with God.

Do we occasionally become sidetracked and pray as if planting more churches, digging more wells, treating more sick and the other items on *our* 'want' list are ends in themselves? We must, as Jesus did, respond to human need. We gain the right to teach the Living Word when we tender physical help in Christ's name to those who hurt and hunger. But all such works of compassion gain significance in the measure to which they prepare people to respond spiritually to God through Jesus Christ. Our prayer and ministry should reflect God's 'want' list.

It is also God's will that Christians come to maturity in Christ. Paul repeatedly challenged the early churches along this line (see Romans 8:29; 1 Corinthians 2:16; Ephesians 4:13, 23-24; Colossians 3:10). Our heart cry and prayer for the worldwide Church is that it might be like Jesus, pure as He is.

"Lord, Teach Us to Pray" (Luke 11:1)

The ministry training team and I were finally in the jeep and the doors were closed! We were setting out on another gospel mission. As was our custom, we paused to pray before I had even started the motor. That day I led in prayer, committing our travel and our day of ministry to the Lord.

After I had finished, Pendy, accustomed to our TEE technique of in-service evaluation, asked, "Was that right praying?" I did a quick mental review of my prayer. As far as I could recall, the prayer was proper.

"What were you thinking about in particular?" I asked, swallowing pride and a slight desperation that came from not remembering everything I had said to the Lord.

"Well, I was thinking of where you said, 'Be with us, Lord.' I hear that in church a lot. Is He with us or isn't He?" Pendy cited verses he and his fellow students had memorized assuring them of God's presence.

"Hmmm. Prayer language, I suppose," I commented, hoping to fill the conversationless hole around us. "Good question! What do the rest of you say to that?"

Silence. We were, after all, in the habit of praying those words. Finally Pendy spoke again.

"Suppose I have given you a pen and then you say, 'My brother, please give me a pen.' And then you say it again: 'Please, my brother, I want a pen from you.' At best I would wonder, wouldn't I, about how unaware you were of what I had just given you? At worst I could be insulted that you did not recognize what I had given you as being the very thing you were asking for."

More silence filled the car. That was unusual, for these students were accustomed to interacting, debating, counseling each other in the normal TEE discussion format. Then I realized that they, like me, were learning a new truth. In addition, they were amazed that their missionary had not known this before!

How often since that day I have had to check my language in prayer. While it is true that God measures the thoughts and intents of our hearts (Hebrews 4:2), it is also true that what flows from our hearts is an indicator of the real issues and our real beliefs (Proverbs 4:23). Do I really hear what I am saying to my God?

"I Want Men Everywhere to Lift up Holy Hands" (1 Timothy 2:8)

Nyondo and I were translating the New Testament into the Tsogo language. As we worked our way through First Timothy, we had translated 2:8 using the generic term—mankind— instead of the specific word for men. But we were brought up short when we came to 2:9 and began wondering why Paul says he "also" expects certain behavior of the women.

On the screen of my memory I still see the incredulous look that came over Nyondo's face when we discovered that the "men" of First Timothy 2:8 were really men—males!

"Why?" Nyondo wanted to know. "Why is God addressing this specific order to us men? Why are the men being told to pray? Are there verses where he also tells you women to pray?"

I found none. But I assured Nyondo that it was perfectly correct for women to pray, because all the other injunctions to pray seemed to be generic, addressed to men and women.

Switching from translation to Bible study, we looked at God's leadership role for men in the home and church. Within that context it was not so unusual that the male of the species receive a personalized exhortation to pray. The context of First Timothy 2:8 suggested another reason for the exhortation. Later, in 2:9-15, Paul is challenging women in our various areas of weakness. Is God, by the same token, challenging men in what is for them their area of weakness?

Nyondo left work that afternoon saying, "I will not sleep tonight until I have shown Pastor Joel and other lay leaders what we have seen today."

Sure enough, not long afterward, Pastor Joel's sermon dealt with the role of men in prayer. "We lament the weakness of Tsogo Christians," he said. "We ask why our church is not growing as it ought. We leaders scold and challenge and try to motivate. We men who lead are not obeying God, and then we wonder why the church among the Tsogo is weak!" Pastor Joel challenged the men to meet him for a special prayer meeting not unlike what the Alliance Women were already doing once a week.

In reminiscing a few years later, Pastor Joel recognized that from that point on something "new" began to happen to the church among the Tsogo. He thanked God that He had given the men a will to obey. Prayer is an act of obedience. It is a special injunction addressed to "men everywhere"—to the sent ones, to those of the sending church and to those of the receiving church.

" 'Ask the Lord of the Harvest . . . to Send Out Workers into His Harvest Field' " (Luke 10:2)

I have had the privilege of being a missionary with The Christian and Missionary Alliance since 1964. As an Alliance missionary, I have participated in a number of homeland missionary conferences.

Wanting the able-bodied in the congregations to

become "go-ers" and all to become givers and prayers, we missionaries work up rich and varied programs. We try to be good orators. We stir up enthusiasm. We motivate. We challenge. We work for excellence in every part of our presentations.

The work of God's kingdom deserves excellence and enthusiasm. But do we depend too much on our own powers to send forth the workers into God's harvest? *Are we spending as much effort praying the Lord of the harvest to send out workers into His harvest field?* Do we feel the same urgency to pray for mothers and fathers to release their sons and daughters for overseas ministry?

Receiving churches are not exempted from this aspect of prayer. How often I have heard national colleagues pray for the churches in North America to send more workers overseas. When I have reminded them that God is the primary Sender, their prayers have changed focus. They have begun to ask God to send people from their own families into the ministry to help alleviate the worker shortage.

Our exciting missionary conferences need to be bathed in prayer. Only in that way can they serve to educate and sensitize God's people to His work around the world. The Holy Spirit does not work in a vacuum. When people are informed, God can readily convince them to act on behalf of worldwide needs. Missionary conferences thus provide an arena in which the Holy Spirit can place in human hearts an intense inner conviction or "call" to service. But prayer remains a key element.

Isaiah 6:1-9 gives us insight into another aspect of praying for laborers. The Godhead asks, "Whom shall I send? And who will go for us?" Isaiah, now within hearing distance and already cleansed from his sin and guilt (6:5-7), responds. Should not we, instead of pleading for workers, pray God to put potential workers within "calling distance"? Do we dare pray specifically that mothers and fathers will hear God calling them to be parents of "sent ones" to any spot on the globe?

Conclusion

Praying in the context of missions means we are networking with thousands of others who have also committed themselves to a working relationship with God. We embrace each other around the globe. We bear mutual burdens He gives us. We share common experiences and rewards. Yet our focus is not on each other or on the work we do together. We focus on "our God, / who sits on the throne, / and [on] the Lamb" (Revelation 7:10).

In *Born for Battle*, R.A. Matthews speaks of the significance of "our" in the opening phrase of the Lord's prayer.

. . . We are probably better acquainted with the horizontal significance of the plural noun, "our." It reaches out to include "all saints" as we seek in prayer the will of the higher relationship at the throne for those bound up with us on the earth level in the family relationship of the Church on earth. It is in the outworking of this ministry that I find myself linking hands with God's saints in China or Cambodia, Mongolia or Mindanao, sharing in their problems and pleadings for them as guided by the Holy Spirit. (pp. 87–88)

As I said earlier, and repeat now, prayer is cross-cultural and multi-cultural in practice and in results. It is supra-cultural as, far above and beyond all culture, each believer in his/her place in the heavenlies is seated with Christ, exercising spiritual authority.

Prayer is the ultimate in missionary action.

Miss Julie Fehr is an Alliance missionary on furlough. Her field is Gabon, Equatorial Africa.

	Fasting, the
CHAPTER	Delightful
	Discipline
7	
	by K. Neill Foster

FASTING, THE DELIGHTFUL DIS-
CIPLINE. Is this a contradiction in
terms? Not so. Fasting can be truly rewarding in the
life of a Christian. Fasting is geared for results. Far
from somber truth dressed in drabness, fasting is a
vibrant, radiant, yes, delightful Christian discipline.

But let's begin with an uncomfortable quotation
from John Wesley, the founder of Methodism, in
1789.

It would be easy to show in many respects the
Methodists in general are deplorably wanting in
the practice of Christian self-denial. While we
were at Oxford, the rule of every Methodist was
to fast every Wednesday and Friday in imitation
of the primitive church.

Now this practice of the primitive church was
universally allowed. "Who does not know," says

Epiphanius, an ancient writer, "that the fast of the fourth and sixth days of the week are observed by the Christians throughout the world?" So they were by the Methodists for several years, by them all without exception. . . . The man who never fasts is no more on the way to heaven than the man who never prays.

I must hasten to say that I do not wholly agree with Wesley's statement about a failure to fast keeping one out of heaven, because it cannot be backed up biblically. Nevertheless, it is fascinating that such a great man of God should make such an extreme statement about fasting. I take it that Wesley wanted no one to be in doubt about his opinion regarding this discipline. Possibly he used an extreme statement to make a needed emphasis and was not concerned that all he said about fasting be taken literally.

I have also heard fasting described as "the quickest way to get anything from God." I think that is absolutely true, though I would like to rephrase the statement to say, "Fasting is the quickest way to get yourself into the position where God can give you what He has wanted to give you all along!"

The late Dr. A.W. Tozer put it this way, "I fast just often enough to let my stomach know who's boss."

But what of the Scripture? The Bible has a great

deal to say about fasting. Some of it is exceedingly interesting—and some of it differs considerably from some popular ideas concerning this delightful but neglected discipline.

Eighty Days for Moses

First, Moses practiced fasting (Exodus 24:18; 34:28; Deuteronomy 9:9, 18). On two occasions he fasted 40 days without food or water, clearly supernatural fasts. The supernatural element is not the absence of food, but the absence of water. Ordinarily, a man without water will die in 10 days. In addition, in Moses' case, the fasts were back to back, which means that if there was no break, Moses went 80 days without food or water. If this is the case, then Moses' 80 days without food was certainly supernatural. If Moses' fasting had been specified as the pattern for us, we could not hope to fast at all apart from God's supernatural intervention.

The human result from Moses' fasting was the reception of God's law among men, an event without parallel and nearly without equal in all of human history. The fasting played a significant part.

I cannot help but wonder what great events never happen because of our aversion to fasting.

Variations

Elijah, too, was a man of the fast (1 Kings 19:8).

Forty days and nights he went on the strength of his last meal. But the same statement, by its omission of any reference to drink, implies that Elijah did not abstain from liquids throughout the 40-day period.

And that in turn presents the possibility of variations in fasting: supernatural—like that of Moses—or natural—like that of Elijah (for it is well known that nearly everyone is able to abstain from food for 40 days and live). Also, continuing to drink water while abstaining from food clearly demonstrates that fasts indeed are varied.

Elijah's ministry was dominated by the miraculous. There can be no substitute for the miraculous in the life of a Christian and fasting will unleash the supernatural.

Do you need a miracle? Fasting could be the door through which it will come.

Daniel's Diet

Daniel's experience with fasting is fascinating (Daniel 9:3; 10:3). He fasted personally for 21 days. And apparently his fast was partial. He ate no pleasant bread nor flesh and drank no wine. But the Scripture stops short of saying he did not eat. From other references in the book of Daniel, it is possible to say that Daniel may have continued his simple diet. But he was fasting all the same, even if he was eating. Today, we would be inclined to call it dieting.

I do not know if you have noticed or not, but as we have probed the Scriptures, fasting has become more and more understandable and feasible. About this point some of you are asking, "Is it not a little much that this writer suggests that one can fast and eat at the same time?"

When I began to notice this possibility in Daniel, I went scurrying to a Bible dictionary. The definition was simple and clear. Fasting is a partial or total abstinence from food and/or water. Others had seen it before!

Perhaps you cannot fast for many days. How about a few hours? Perhaps a partial fast will exactly meet your needs.

When you discover that it is possible to eat and fast at the same time, you are beginning to discover just how versatile fasting really is as a spiritual weapon. If fasting really is a spiritual weapon, anyone should be able to pick it up at any time and wield it in his own circumstances. And that is exactly the case.

Grass-Roots Fasting

The book of Jonah teaches about fasting as well. First, observe that the people proclaimed a fast and the king supported it. Evidently the initiative for fasting can come from the grass roots as well as from those in authority. In the case of the Ninevites, the fast was total and even the animals were included. It lasted for three days and three nights and it was linked with repentance. Perhaps the greatest revival recorded in Scripture follows. The result was the salvation of a nation. And these Ninevites were not even acknowledged followers of Jehovah!

Can fasting be effective even when practiced by unbelievers? The Bible implies that it is possible. And if God answers the prayers of unconverted people (compare Acts 10 and 11 in the life of Cornelius), then why should God not honor the fasting of a repentant people?

National Deliverance

The story of Esther demonstrates that a leader may also call a fast (Esther 4:16). Queen Esther called for a fast and all the people were obligated to cooperate. The fast was total for three days and three nights. But the Jews were delivered; the massacre of a nation was averted through the discipline of fasting.

In the New Testament, we read that Paul was in *fastings* (2 Corinthians 6:5). Note the plural. It is not surprising that our Christian experiences are not like those of Paul. Our fasting is not like his, either. Paul also says he was in fastings *often* (2 Corinthians 11:27). Frequent fasting has an obvious connection with spiritual power. But for most of us it is a connection that has been broken.

Fasting without Hunger

In 2 Corinthians 11:27 (". . . in hunger and thirst, in fastings often") a fascinating truth about fasting comes to the fore. Paul distinguishes between hungerings and fastings. And if there truly is a difference between being hungry and fasting, then one of the most common objections to fasting is circumvented.

I recall looking forward with anticipation to a break in my evangelistic schedule. I wanted to fast for a few days. And can you imagine my delight when I discovered that from the very first there was no hunger?

Going hungry is one thing. Fasting is another. And once we learn that, fasting becomes an even more attractive and practical discipline. On the other hand, sometimes I find that I want to fast but cannot because I am too hungry, possibly because the Holy Spirit is not prompting the fast. But there are other times, when God wants me to fast, that it becomes to me the wholly delightful discipline that it is.

Our Lord and Savior, like Moses and Elijah, also fasted 40 days. It is significant that He did this before His ministry began and before the miraculous began to occur. The absence of the miraculous among many of today's Christians could be traceable to the lack of this forgotten discipline.

I think it is also safe to assume that although Jesus

did not eat for 40 days, He did drink water. An indication of this is that Satan tempted Him on the point of eating, not drinking—on the point of hunger, not thirst.

Fasting Alone

In Matthew 6, three fascinating promises are given (vv. 4, 6, 18). Christ says, "Pray, give and fast in secret and God will reward you openly" (paraphrase). Fasting is here presented as a spiritual force in its own right. Praying brings results. Giving brings results. And fasting, by itself, brings results too.

Apart from prayer? Yes, apart from prayer. The promise which accompanies fasting is not hinged to prayer. It is hinged to fasting alone. Mind you, prayer and fasting are repeatedly linked in the Scripture. They are powerful twins in the spiritual warfare, but they are not Siamese twins. Together they multiply the release of spiritual power. But alone as well, fasting brings results.

Now any Christian would be foolish indeed to argue against praying. Far from it. But a word in favor of fasting needs to be spoken. A telephone operator, for example, who talks in her work, could be occupied completely with her job and could still apply tremendous spiritual force to a personal problem through fasting. And if she can maintain an attitude of prayer throughout, all the better.

Missionary Fasting

Fasting in the book of Acts played a vital role in the commissioning of missionaries and in what we might now call church business meetings (Acts 13:1–4). Today we tend to schedule banquets when the church's business is to be done. Could that be why it is so poorly done sometimes? Could our lack of fasting have any relationship to the lack of missionary candidates?

Probably the greatest text on the subject of fasting is found in Isaiah 58:6, KJV. After a five-verse description of the type of fast God does not like, the prophet says, "Is not this the fast that I have chosen, to loose the bands of wickedness, to undo the heavy burdens and to let the oppressed go free, and that ye break every yoke?"

Fasting will loose the bands of wickedness. And there are plenty of those.

Fasting will undo the heavy burdens. And there is no shortage of burdened people.

Fasting will free the oppressed. And to me this is a clear reference to the liberation of those bound by Satan. Occult bondage is shattered by fasting. Sometimes nothing else will break through.

Every Yoke

Fasting also will break every yoke. Thank God for that *every*. For example, an invisible yoke is often formed between young couples, one a believer and the other not. Concerned parents talk and cajole. But arguments only push the young people together. Fasting is what is needed to break a yoke like that. And fasting can be applied to a problem without the participation or even the knowledge of the principals involved. Why, oh why, have we allowed the ruin of so many of our homes and families without ever once unsheathing the yoke-splintering fast which God has given us? The answer is not so easy.

Christ made it clear that while He was present on earth His disciples would not fast, though the followers of John the Baptist, of course, did fast. But Jesus also made it clear that after He departed, His disciples would fast (Mark 2:19–20). I believe that at Christ's return fasting by the church will be terminated. But now, in the meantime, fasting is God's order. A non-fasting church is out of order!

In any discussion of fasting some reference needs to be made to 1 Corinthians 7:5, KJV, "Defraud ye not one the other, except it be with consent for a time, that ye may give yourselves to fasting and prayer."

The context clearly indicates that a temporary abstinence from sexual relations within marriage is a fitting and proper self-discipline.

One of my friends in the ministry describes fasting this way: "Fasting is a disciplined abstinence from all that gratifies or satisfies the flesh in order to give one's self totally to seeking the Lord in the Spirit. This is the ultimate. Anything less is partial."

A fast may be undertaken in secret, as in Matthew 6, or it may be public, as in Acts 13. It may be initiated by a leader, as in Esther, or it may come from the grass roots, as in Nineveh. It may be done carnally, with wrong motives, and without effect. But if Christ truly lives in the Church and in us, He is the same Savior who fasted 40 days. And He wishes to express His fasting nature through us today so that He can hone the spirituality and discernment of His church.

Some say, "I believe in fasting, but I don't feel led." It is true that we should be led as God's children. But why is it that so few Christians are led to fast when it is so obviously a vital part of Christianity? Usually, we fail to fast because the whole concept of fasting has remained uninviting and uninspiring. Fasting has not been presented as a wholly delightful discipline. But that is what it is!

Always Results

At this point I would like to say that I have never fasted without seeing some result. When I shared this fact with a friend who is a pastor, he countered with, "But when I fast, nothing ever happens."

However, we fasted together one day during a campaign and that evening the church was full. A film was shown which had a very ordinary impact. My message was ordinary enough, though evangelistic and clear. But God was there. There were many inquirers. Men, women, young people and children. So many went to the inquiry room that we lost track of how many had responded.

The next day I asked my pastor friend, "Can you still say that God never does anything when we fast?"

With a smile, he answered, "No!"

A Last Word

Enthusiasm for fasting is understandable. But the pitfall of regularly scheduled fasts should probably be avoided. All biblical fasts were issue-oriented. A determination to fast every Monday or the third Thursday, for example, may lead present-day believers into the kind of fasting the Bible consistently condemns. It is far better, I think, to apply the awesome power of fasting to specific issues at specific times. The results are certain to be gratifying indeed.

Dr. K. Neill Foster is the Executive Vice-President/Publisher of Christian Publications, Inc., in Camp Hill, Pennsylvania.

The
Four-Fold
Gospel

Who may ascend the hill of the LORD?
Who may stand in his holy place?
He who has clean hands and a pure heart,
who does not lift up his soul to an idol
or swear by what is false.
(Psalm 24:3–4)

Create in me a pure heart, O God,
and renew a steadfast spirit within me.
Do not cast me from your presence
or take your Holy Spirit from me.
Restore to me the joy of your salvation
and grant me a willing spirit, to sustain me.
Then I will teach transgressors your ways,
and sinners will turn back to you.
(Psalm 51:10–13)

If I had cherished sin in my heart,
the Lord would not have listened.
(Psalm 66:18)

	The Salvation
CHAPTER	Prayer
8	*by Richard W. Bailey*

WHY A CHAPTER ON PRAYER for salvation? Is not the penitent's prayer, "God be merciful to me, a sinner," sufficient? Did not the thief on the cross simply cry out, "Remember me when You come into Your kingdom"? Is the prayer for salvation so complicated that it takes a whole chapter to explain it?

Salvation is all God's work, manifested in Christ. Whether it is a confession of our need, an illumination of our understanding or faith to believe in the atoning work of Christ, everything in salvation has its source in God. If it is all of God, and God does not want anyone to perish but everyone to come to repentance, why is it that two billion people in our present world have not been saved? Why this apparent contradiction?

Although salvation is the completed work of God, He has ordained that prayer must be expressed by every individual person in order to experience salvation. " 'For, everyone who calls on the name of the Lord will be saved' " (Romans 10:13). This is a mystery, but a truth revealed that demands clear understanding. It is this prayer for salvation that occupies the theme of this chapter.

The prayer for salvation is a composite of at least three essential ingredients: 1) the prayer for salvation is a prayer of confession; 2) the prayer for salvation is a prayer of repentance; and 3) the prayer for salvation is a prayer of acceptance. Too often the church is full of professing Christians whose lifestyles, attitudes and conversations indicate they have never understood or experienced the prayer of faith for salvation. The lifestyle of the world and the lifestyle of the church often become hard to distinguish. Is it possible that there may be professing Christians in our churches who have never really prayed the authentic salvation prayer?

The Prayer for Salvation Is a Prayer of Confession

What is confession? Too many times we equate confession with a recital of known sins. We go before a priest, clergyman or Christian friend and confess our sins. Scriptures, however, also give the term *confession* a legal connotation. It is used primarily when a person testifies to a fact or agrees that what is said is true. In this sense he or she makes a confession. The word was often used in the courts and in legal matters to declare or to affirm an objective. While the word is used in Scripture on some occasions in relation to the confessing of sins, its thought is always to declare the verdict of truth about our sins.

Prayer for salvation begins with a confession that we are sinners and that Christ is our only Savior. We confess that there is no forgiveness of sin apart from His shed blood on the cross. We confess that Jesus Christ is the only way to be reconciled to God. Prayer for salvation does not begin with going to an altar or a booth, or sitting in a circle, confessing our specific sins. This may have some psychological value, but this practice is sure to overlook sins we are neither ready to confess nor anxious to have exposed. Prayer for salvation begins by our confessing that our very nature is sinful. There is no good thing in us. Christ is the only righteous one and He alone can be our Savior. Confession is not salvation, but confession leads us to Christ who is our Savior.

The church has many confessional creeds; we may be familiar with a few of them. Perhaps we can recite the *Apostles' Creed* and are acquainted with the *Nicene Creed*, the *Augsburg Confession* and the *Westminster Confession*. However comprehensive these confessions, they do not bring salvation to anyone. The tragedy is that many churches have equated salvation with a creedal confession.

Next Sunday thousands of persons will recite the *Apostles' Creed*. Most will do so in the false belief that affirming Christ's death and resurrection is all they need to do to be saved. Christ has died for all sinners, they reason, and therefore all sinners are saved. They believe the mission of the Church is simply to let people know that Christ is Savior. Such belief questions the depravity of mankind and the lostness of those who have never once heard the good news of the gospel. They suppose a loving God would not exclude those who have never heard.

Confession of truth is necessary, but confession is not salvation. "It is with your heart that you believe and are justified, and it is with your mouth that you confess and are saved" (Romans 10:10). Jesus said, " 'Not everyone who says to me, "Lord, Lord," will enter the kingdom of heaven . . .' " (Matthew 7:21). Some will confess that they have done great miracles in Christ's name and Jesus will say, " 'I never knew you' " (Matthew 7:23). There is a day coming when every knee will bow before Christ and every tongue will confess to God; but this is judgment, not salvation.

The prayer of confession is an essential ingredient, but in Christ alone is salvation for those who confess they are sinners.

The Prayer of Salvation Is a Prayer of Repentance

Sorrow for sin is common, but repentance is more than sorrow. It includes a need for change in our moral character. Sorrow alone, however we express it, does not in and of itself constitute repentance. Most everyone is sorry for his or her sin. Even Judas was deeply sorrowful for betraying Jesus. Repentance necessitates a change of heart and mind. Not only change about our choices, our purposes, our intentions, but change about ourselves. Most people want to get rid of the bad things in their lives, but few in this day of emphasis on self-fulfillment want to get rid of themselves.

Nevertheless Jesus said, " 'If anyone would be my disciple, he must deny himself, take up his cross daily and follow me' " (Luke 9:23). Repentance is turning self-effort, self-goodness, self-purposes to God's purposes and God's salvation. Repentance is understanding that self-centeredness is sin, that our wrong deeds and actions are a result of self-centeredness or independence from God.

The Church often spends much time counseling people how to get rid of bad habits and bad attitudes. The problem is, when we get rid of one bad habit another lifts its ugly head. We have been trying to disciple people into salvation rather than disciple people after salvation. The prayer for salvation includes repentance that turns a person from a totally depraved self to a totally holy God through our Savior, Jesus Christ. There will be sorrow for sin, but there will be a loathing of ourselves as morally bankrupt and a prayer for deliverance from our sinful selves. True repentance is a total change of heart, a complete turning from ourselves to Himself. True repentance lifts us from discouragement and despondency to hope in Christ alone. True repentance is not a transitory act, but an abiding principle to be carried out throughout life.

Paul's message concerning the apostolic age was very simple: " 'They must turn to God in repentance and have faith in our Lord Jesus' " (Acts 20:21). The message that Jesus proclaimed was, " 'Repent for the kingdom of heaven in near' " (Matthew 4:17). And again, " 'Unless you repent you . . . will . . . perish' " (Luke 13:3). Repentance leads us to Christ, who alone is our salvation.

The Prayer for Salvation Is a Prayer of Acceptance

It is not through embracing some special teaching or the recitation of the Four Spiritual Laws or even confession or repentance that we are saved; Jesus Christ alone saves us. "To all who received him, to those who believed in his name, he gave the right to become children of God" (John 1:12). Jesus said, " 'I am the way and the truth and the life' " (John 14:6). The way to salvation is through the prayer of repentance, the truth of salvation is through the prayer of confession, and the life of salvation is through the prayer of acceptance.

We must receive into our lives Christ Jesus as Savior and Lord: "If anyone is in Christ, he is a new creation" (2 Corinthians 5:17). Only when we are in Christ is there salvation. Salvation is not in the Church, not in creeds, not in our good deeds; it is in Christ alone.

We are saved by His life: "For if, when we were God's enemies, we were reconciled to him through the death of his Son, how much more, having been reconciled, shall we be saved through his life!" (Romans 5:10).

There is salvation in no other name: " 'Salvation is found in no one else, for there is no other name under heaven given to men by which we must be saved' " (Acts 4:12).

Christ is our only way to God: "There is one God and one mediator between God and men, the man Christ Jesus" (1 Timothy 2:5).

Apart from Christ there is no forgiveness: "In him we have redemption through his blood, the forgiveness of sins, in accordance with the riches of God's grace" (Ephesians 1:7).

It is in Christ we are washed, we are sanctified, and we are justified: "But you were washed, you were sanctified, you were justified in the name of the Lord Jesus Christ and by the Spirit of our God" (1 Corinthians 6:11).

No language, no natural logic, no human understanding, no self-improvement will suffice. Jesus Christ alone is our Savior. The prayer for salvation comes through the regenerating work of the Holy

Spirit. This is a radical happening. Jesus explained it to Nicodemus as a "new birth" (John 3:5). In this new life, "the old has gone, the new has come!" (2 Corinthians 5:17). " 'This is eternal life [salvation], that they may know you, the only true God, and Jesus Christ, whom you have sent' " (John 17:3).

Conclusion

When we say that Christ is our Savior, we are acknowledging that God initiated and completed the work of salvation through His Son, Jesus Christ. We are saying that God purposed from before the foundation of the world that Christ alone is our mediator, Christ alone is the propitiation for our sins, Christ alone is our justification, and Christ alone is our Savior. When we speak of the prayer for salvation, we are acknowledging that we are free moral beings who may choose to confess, may choose to repent and may choose to accept into our lives Christ as Savior and Lord. The fact is, salvation can have no personal meaning or redemptive power apart from the prayer for salvation.

Dr. Richard W. Bailey is Vice President of Church Ministries for The Christian and Missionary Alliance.

CHAPTER	"Holy Spirit,
	Fill Me!"
9	
	by Fred A. Hartley, III

I T IS THE MOST THRILLING moment in the life of any Christian when he or she genuinely prays, "Holy Spirit, fill me!" Such a moment is preceded by an increased appetite for spiritual growth.

Spiritual hunger is a sign of spiritual vitality. The deep inner desire for a growing relationship with God motivates us in the right direction.

Jesus said, "Blessed are those who hunger and thirst for righteousness for they will be filled" (Matthew 5:6).

David said, "As the deer pants for the streams of water, so my soul pants for you, O God" (Psalm 42:1).

Isaiah said, "Come, all you who are thirsty" (Isaiah 55:1).

Jeremiah said, "When your words came, I ate them" (Jeremiah 15:16).

And as it relates to our deep desire to be filled with the Holy Spirit, A.W. Tozer said, "No one has ever been filled with the Holy Spirit who didn't first believe he could be filled with the Holy Spirit."

My own spiritual hunger was awakened when I was in college. I read the Bible but it was as dry as nibbling on sawdust. I prayed but my prayers seemed to fall back to the ground. I wanted to serve but my efforts seemed impotent. My soul felt strangely barren and I was distressed because I knew it was not normal.

During that time a dear black woman in our church came up to me each week and said, "Fred, I'm praying for you." I would thank her. Then again the following week, "Fred, I'm praying for you."

Finally I asked, "What exactly are you praying for me?"

She beamed as if she knew a secret and said, "That you receive the gift."

"Oh," I replied, "you must mean the gift of tongues and the Holy Spirit. I already have the Holy Spirit because I'm a Christian and He doesn't always give the gift of tongues to everyone."

Rather than arguing, she simply beamed and reminded me, "Fred, I'm praying for you."

Each week this continued until I finally was provoked to ask her, "Go ahead and pray for me; just don't tell me anymore. *I ALREADY HAVE THE HOLY SPIRIT.*"

Then she innocently asked, "You have the Holy Spirit; but does the Holy Spirit have you?" Ouch!

I continued to argue with her but she again asked me a valid question, "If you are right and I am wrong, then how come you're the one getting all upset?" She had me cornered!

This dear woman's prayers and my own deep hunger for the fullness of the Holy Spirit led me on a wonderful spiritual pilgrimage I would like to share with you.

Strange Ideas

Many of us have strange ideas about the Holy Spirit.

As a new Christian, I attended a teenage Bible study at which the leader asked an opening question to a group of approximately 50 students that was designed to stimulate discussion. "Who do you think the Holy Spirit is?"

I immediately raised my hand and blurted out, "He's sort of like the Wizard of Oz—you know what I mean, like a giant computer . . . like a nuclear power plant in the sky."

My poor Bible study teacher almost dropped his dentures. The more I tried to elaborate, the more the discussion got off track. "The Holy Spirit is sort of like electricity, raw power—like the Force in *Star Wars*." My concept of the Holy Spirit was so mistaken I don't think my poor youth pastor ever did get that Bible study back on track. Fortunately, my concept has since then been corrected by careful

Bible teaching.

As we get to know the Holy Spirit, perhaps the most important thing we need to learn about Him is that He is a *Person*. Far more than simply being a power or an impersonal force, He is just as much a real live, distinct person as you and I.

The Holy Spirit has feelings.
He has affections (Romans 15:30).
He gets sad (Ephesians 4:30).
He experiences rejection (Hebrews 10:29).

The Holy Spirit has a will.
He gives gifts (1 Corinthians 12:11).
He speaks (Acts 13:2).
He rebukes, corrects and guides (Acts 16:6–7).
He commands (Acts 8:29).
He leads (Romans 8:14).

The Holy Spirit has thoughts.
He teaches (John 14:26).
He witnesses (Romans 8:27).
He prays (Romans 8:26).
He searches our hearts and minds
    (1 Corinthians 2:10–11).

The Holy Spirit has desires.
He calls people into service (Acts 13:2).

He convicts and convinces people
(John 16:8–11).

Once we understand that the Holy Spirit is a Person, we certainly want to understand that He is the *Divine* Person. He is fully God. Everything God does, the Holy Spirit does. There is after all only one God who has eternally existed in three Persons—Father, Son and Holy Spirit—each of whom are fully equal in divine essence.

In addition, the Holy Spirit is the *indwelling* Divine Person. Every Christian has the Holy Spirit living inside of him or her. The Bible says, "Anyone who does not have the Spirit of Christ, . . . does not belong to Christ" (Romans 8:9). When we become Christians we often say that we "receive Christ" and that Jesus lives inside of us. However, if we get X-rayed, Jesus Christ will not show up on the picture. When we bleed, we do not bleed Jesus. Christ is inside us, not physically, but by virtue of His Holy Spirit. With this basic understanding of *who* the Holy Spirit is, we now want to understand *what* He does.

The Primary Function

Many Christians are confused about the primary function of the Holy Spirit. Some people insist that the primary function of the Holy Spirit is to give the gift of speaking in tongues. Others insist that the primary function of the Holy Spirit is to give us power in witnessing. Others suggest that He exists to make us happy inside.

The Bible teaches that the Holy Spirit's primary job is to make Jesus known. Jesus Himself said, "When the Counselor [Holy Spirit] comes, . . . he will testify about me" (John 15:26). A great Bible teacher of the last generation, F.B. Myers, was very perceptive when he said, "He is like a shaft of light that falls on the beloved face of Jesus, so that as in the photograph you do not think about the light or the origin of the light, but you think about the face that it reveals."

We see the Holy Spirit function this way in the virgin birth. God the Father impregnated Mary with God the Son when she was overshadowed by the Holy Spirit (see Luke 1:35). The Holy Spirit actually activated the ovum of Mary so Christ might be conceived.

We see the Holy Spirit function this way in the life and ministry of John the Baptist. Since this prophet was sent to have the unique ministry of being a forerunner of Christ, leading the way for Him, it is not surprising that he was actually filled with the Holy Spirit prior to his birth (see Luke 1:41).

We see the Holy Spirit function this way in the creation of the world. It was God the Father who spoke the six divine fiats (Genesis 1:1); it was the eternal Word (the Son) who came forth from the

Father (John 1:1–3); but it was the Spirit who activated the Word and brought the world into being (Genesis 1:2).

We see the Holy Spirit function this way in the life of every believer. When an individual begins to seek Christ, it is the Holy Spirit drawing him or her to Christ (John 6:44). When that individual chooses Christ and is actually born again, it is the Holy Spirit who has accomplished this work (John 3:6–8). And when that person continues to grow in Christ, in prayer and in obedience, it is the Holy Spirit who is enabling (Romans 8:26–27; Zechariah 4:6).

Let's review.

The Holy Spirit is a *Person*.

He is the *Divine* Person.

He is the *indwelling* Divine Person.

He is the indwelling Divine Person whose *primary purpose is to make Jesus known to us*.

In addition, He is the *invisible*, indwelling Divine Person. Because He is invisible, we are often completely unaware of His presence. And because He is very much a gentleman, He will not force His way on us.

A Valid Question

Since the Holy Spirit is invisible and lives inside of us all the time, whether we realize it or not, we are constantly relating to Him. At times we are treating

Him with respect and tragically at other times we are treating Him with great disrespect.

A question that is worth asking as a daily habit is, "*Holy Spirit, how am I treating you?*" The Bible teaches that there are several ways we can mistreat the Holy Spirit.

(1) The Bible says it is possible to "grieve the Holy Spirit" (Ephesians 4:30). To grieve means to cause Him sorrow, to offend Him, to hurt His feelings. When we grieve the Holy Spirit it is because we have committed some level of active sin such as dishonesty, lying, bad attitudes and sharp words. The Holy Spirit will not leave us, but as a gentleman, He will not force His way on us and will perhaps even withdraw His positive influence. Whenever we grieve the Holy Spirit, we sin against God.

(2) The Bible also teaches it is possible to "quench the Holy Spirit" (1 Thessalonians 5:19, KJV). To quench means to "douse the fire." The New International Version translates that verse "Do not put out the Spirit's fire." Frequently in the Bible the Holy Spirit is referred to as fire. The Holy Spirit comes into our lives to consume us with a fervent love for Christ. He wants us to read the Bible, to pray, to share our faith with others, to praise the Lord regardless of circumstance. When we refuse to obey Him and squelch His desires, it's like dousing a fire with water. We grieve the Holy Spirit through

active sin—doing things we are told not to do. We quench the Holy Spirit through passive sin—not doing things we were told to do.

Filled with the Spirit

Obviously on the negative side, we are not to grieve or quench the Holy Spirit. On the positive side, from the moment a person receives the invisible, indwelling Divine Person of the Holy Spirit, the Holy Spirit has one ultimate desire—to fill us to overflowing.

The Bible says, "Do not get drunk on wine, which leads to debauchery. Instead, be filled with the Spirit" (Ephesians 5:18). Being filled with the Holy Spirit is not an experience God delegates to only a few super-Christians; rather, it is an experience He has promised to all of His children.

Billy Graham states it bluntly, "I believe the greatest need today is for men and women who believe in the name of Jesus Christ to be filled with the Holy Spirit. If you are not filled with the Holy Spirit, you are sinning against God."

There are over 30,000 promises in God's Word. We claim them frequently. But there is only one that is called "the promise of the Father." Jesus told His disciples, "Do not leave Jerusalem, but wait for the gift my Father promised" (Acts 1:4). Again He told His disciples, "I am going to send you what my Father has promised; but stay in the city until you have been clothed with power from on high" (Luke 24:49).

Then on the day of Pentecost, Peter stood up and quoted Joel's prophecy which was initially fulfilled when God poured out His Holy Spirit upon the first-century believers, " 'In the last days,' God says, 'I will pour out my Spirit on all people. Your sons and daughters will prophesy, your young men will see visions, your old men will dream dreams' " (Acts 2:17). After they were all filled with the Holy Spirit, Peter preached and 3,000 were saved. He told them, "Repent and be baptized, every one of you, in the name of Jesus Christ for the forgiveness of your sins. And you will receive the gift of the Holy Spirit. The promise is for you and your children and for all who are far off" (2:38–39).

My Testimony

I will never forget the date February 1, 1975. As a result of my own deep spiritual hunger and the prayers of a dear black woman, I got down on my knees in our living room and made sure that no one else was home and that the door was locked. I had previously "totally committed" my life to Christ a thousand times. In fact, I was so committed I was blue in the face. My commitment was based almost entirely on my own self-effort. Now something different was happening. Not only was I totally surrendering to Christ, but now for the first time I was totally receiving all there was for me in His Spirit. I told God I knew it was wrong to seek an emotional experience, to demand any particular spiritual gift including the gift of tongues, but on the other hand I was convinced that He promised me that I could be filled with all the fullness of the Holy Spirit and that there was nothing wrong with claiming by faith the promise of the Father. I quoted the following verses in prayer:

Be filled with the Spirit. (Ephesians 5:18)
If you then, though you are evil, know how to give good gifts to your children, how much more will your Father in heaven give the Holy Spirit to those who ask him! (Luke 11:13)
For John baptized with water, but in a few days you will be baptized with the Holy Spirit. . . . But you will receive power when the Holy Spirit comes on you; and you will be my witnesses . . . (Acts 1:5, 8)
Does God give you his Spirit and work miracles among you because you observe the law or because you believe what you heard? (Galatians 3:5)
After they prayed, the place where they were meeting was shaken. And they were all filled with the Holy Spirit and spoke the word of God boldly. (Acts 4:31)
"If anyone is thirsty, let him come to me and

drink. . . . As the Scripture has said, streams of living water will flow from within him." By this he meant the Spirit. (John 7:37–39)

Then I prayed a prayer very similar to this:

Jesus, I am grateful to You for my salvation, because Your death and resurrection purchased a place for me in heaven. I was unworthy of Your grace but You gave it freely to me. I know I have eternal life, and I now have a deep longing in my soul to know for certain that I have been filled with the Holy Spirit. I know You have given me this promise. Cleanse me of all sin by the blood of the Lord Jesus Christ. I turn over my entire life to You. And right now, fill me, saturate me—every area of my life, every cell of my body, every thought. Immerse me in the Holy Spirit. I receive this by faith and I will never again doubt whether or not I have been filled. Yes, I know I am filled. Praise You Jesus. Hallelujah!

Very similarly as when I was baptized in water, it was as if I had waded into the baptismal waters of the Holy Spirit and Jesus, my Pastor, immersed me under the water and saturated me with His Spirit. Many times previously I had given my life to God, but I in turn had never before received all of Him.

After I had prayed, I got up off my knees and sat in the chair. I had not been hit with a lightening bolt, but I had a deep assurance that I prayed the prayer Jesus wanted me to pray. By faith I had received the fullness of Christ. I quietly sang a song to Jesus Christ and joy welled up within me.

At that moment I knew for certain that I had been filled with the Holy Spirit. It was not because I had goose bumps or a warm-fuzzy feeling inside. I knew I was filled, not by feeling, but by faith. The Bible said it, I believed it, and that settled it.

Virtually every day I continue to plead the blood of Christ over my body to cleanse me of sin and I ask the Holy Spirit to fill me again, but it was February 1, when I was filled initially.

Seven Changes

Over the next two weeks, seven very distinct changes took place in my life. They happened so rapidly and dramatically, I knew God was responsible. In abbreviated form, here are the seven changes:

(1) A deep conviction of sin was such a heavy burden that I was constrained to make 40 long distance telephone calls receiving forgiveness and making restitution with people I had almost forgotten about.

(2) Praise. Songs and choruses were sung from my

heart to the Lord with great gusto and delight.

(3) Prayer. For the first time God began to ingrain a disciplined prayer life into me, from which I have seen thousands of answers (and hundreds of un-answers)!

(4) Miracles. As I prayed with the faith God gave me, He showed me dramatic responses.

(5) The fruit of the Spirit—love, joy, peace (Galatians 5:22–23)—began to grow in increasing measure. I certainly remain far from a finished product, but consistency has come.

(6) The gifts of the Spirit have been manifested—in ways I never anticipated.

(7) Power in ministry. Both in personal evangelism and in public preaching, people began to respond to the Word of God when presented.

The list is not intended by any means to represent the full extent of the work of the Spirit, but simply to illustrate that when the Holy Spirit fills a life, we can experience a dramatic inner transformation.

This promise of fullness is simply for us as in-dividuals; it is given to all of God's Church.

A Forgotten Promise

Historically, virtually every orthodox Christian denomination held to the importance of the doctrine of being filled with the Holy Spirit, but then lost its grip on the experience.

Several years ago, I read a human interest story in the newspaper telling of a retired man in Hollywood, Florida, who took his life savings and purchased a $100,000 U.S. Government Treasury Bearer Bond. He took the bond to be photocopied, placed the original on top of the machine, inserted his 25 cents, pressed the button, grabbed his copy, walked out and got in his automobile to drive home. Suddenly, he realized his horrifying mistake. He had left the original in the top of the copier. With panic, he hurried back, only to find his life savings had been taken.

Many solid Bible-believing churches have ignorantly committed the same type of mistake; they have exchanged the reality of the promise of the Father for a photocopy.

The Lutherans certainly believed in the infilling of the Holy Spirit. Martin Luther, in his renowned hymn "A Mighty Fortress Is Our God," spoke about how "the Spirit and the gifts are ours."

The Methodists certainly believed in the infilling of the Holy Spirit. John Wesley wrote how he felt his heart "strangely warmed" and went on to say that he saw no place in the ministry for young men who were not filled with the Holy Spirit.

The Presbyterians certainly believed in the infilling of the Holy Spirit. John Calvin called the church "the fellowship of the flaming heart" and wrote about the "baptism of the Spirit and fire."

The Baptists, who looked to Charles Finney, knew about the infilling of the Holy Spirit. Finney's ministry was accompanied by signs and wonders and he prayed to be filled with the Holy Spirit before he preached every sermon.

Even the Fundamentalists, who claim fellowship with R.A. Torrey and D.L. Moody, have historically accepted the experience of being filled with the Holy Spirit. In the small book *Why God Used D.L. Moody*, by Torrey, he explained how Mr. Moody struggled with some of his faculty members:

"Oh why will they split hairs? Why don't they see that this is just the one thing that they themselves need? They are good teachers, they are wonderful teachers, and I am so glad to have them here; but why will they not see that the baptism with the Holy Ghost is just the one touch that they themselves need?"

I shall never forget the eighth of July, 1894, to my dying day. It was the closing day of the Northfield Students' Conference—the gathering of the students from the eastern colleges. Mr. Moody had asked me to preach on Saturday night and Sunday morning on the baptism with the Holy Ghost. On Saturday night I had spoken about, "The Baptism with the Holy Ghost: What It Is; What It Does; The Need of It and the Possibility of It." On Sunday morning I spoke on,

"The Baptism with the Holy Spirit: How to Get It." It was just exactly twelve o'clock when I finished my morning sermon, and I took out my watch and said: "Mr. Moody has invited us all to go up on the mountain at three o'clock this afternoon to pray for the power of the Holy Spirit. It is three hours to three o'clock. Some of you cannot wait three hours. You do not need to wait. Go to your room; go out into the woods; go to your tent; go anywhere you can get alone with God and have this matter out with Him." At three o'clock we all gathered in front of Mr. Moody's mother's house (she was then still living), and then began to pass down the lane, through the gate, up on the mountainside. There were four hundred and fifty-six of us in all; I know the number because Paul Moody counted us as we passed through the gate.

The Christian and Missionary Alliance began with a belief in the experience of being filled with the Holy Spirit. Their founder, Albert Simpson, had been a minister for more than 10 years when in 1875 he knew something was missing. His inner hunger led him to seek God and read anything on personal piety and the person of the Holy Spirit that he could get his hands on. He described his experience:

Throwing myself at the feet of my glorious Master, just at that time God poured out His Spirit upon my own heart. It was then that I received for the first time the new light of the indwelling Christ and the baptism of the Holy Spirit. It became a fire in my bones and so possessed me that nights long I waited before God crying to Him for a great revival.

Soon after this crisis, Simpson organized a citywide evangelistic crusade in Louisville, Kentucky, where he was pastoring. The result: he saw more souls saved then ever before in his ministry—5,000 to 6,000 came to Christ! This was the beginning of a great harvest, and it started with the consecrated life of A.B. Simpson. He was used to begin the great missionary enterprise of The Christian and Missionary Alliance—a missionary organization whose fires still brightly shine today, over a century later.

Many of Simpson's old associates rejected his friendship because of his openness to the fullness of the Holy Spirit, but that was part of the cost. He wanted power rather than popularity, and God mightily used him.

Simpson wrote about the fullness of the indwelling Christ in his popular poem "Himself."

Once it was the blessing, now it is the Lord;
Once it was the feeling, now it is His Word.
Once His gifts I wanted, now the Giver own;
Once I sought for healing, now Himself alone.
Once 'twas painful trying, now 'tis perfect trust;
Once a half salvation, now the uttermost.
Once 'twas ceaseless holding, now He holds me
    fast;
Once 'twas constant drifting, now my anchor's
    cast.
Once 'twas busy planning, now 'tis trustful prayer;
Once 'twas anxious caring, now He has the care.
Once 'twas what I wanted, now what Jesus says;
Once 'twas constant asking, now 'tis ceaseless
    praise.
Once it was my working, His it hence shall be.
Once I tried to use Him, now He uses me.
Once the power I wanted, now the Mighty One;
Once for self I labored, now for Him alone.
Once I hoped in Jesus, now I know He's mine;
Once my lamps were dying, now they brightly
    shine.
Once for death I waited, now His coming hail;
And my hopes are anchored, safe within the veil.

Even today The Christian and Missionary Alliance includes as one of the 11 points to its Statement of Faith:

It is the will of God that each believer should be filled with the Holy Spirit and be sanctified wholly, being separated from sin and the world and fully dedicated to the will of God, thereby receiving power for holy living and effective service. This is both a crisis and a progressive experience wrought in the life of the believer subsequent to conversion.

Like many denominations and groups, we do not want to tragically lose our grip on the promise of the Father in exchange for a cheap look-alike.

Growing Up

As the church gets older, it needs to be careful it does not forget the promise of the Father.

When I was a small child, my parents gave me a little wind-up train which I loved to play with. I would wind it up, place it on the track, and watch it with fascination make the circle until it ran out of speed. When I got a little older, my parents gave me an electric train that I could sit on the track and work from the transformer all day long. The difference was the electric train was plugged into a constant power source.

As a younger Christian, I was challenged to read the Bible, pray, witness and obey God. I would do so with great aspirations, but would soon come to a dismal and defeated halt. However, as I grew in

Christ, I came to the place in my spiritual life where He taught me that the Christian life is impossible apart from divine enabling. I realized I was not expected to live the Christian life on my own, but I could tap into that constant power source and rely on the invisible indwelling Divine Person of the Holy Spirit.

The Lord Jesus wants to fill us with the Holy Spirit at an initial crisis moment, which we receive by faith, claiming the promises of God just as we did salvation. In addition, He desires to fill us daily and progressively give us power for holy living and effective service.

There are literally thousands of promises in the Bible, but there is only one promise known as "the promise of the Father." It is to be received by faith. Let's remember . . .

- The Holy Spirit is a Person; the indwelling, invisible, Divine Person.
- We do not want to grieve Him or quench Him, but His primary desire is to fill us to overflowing with His wonderful presence.
- He promises us that He will completely fill us when we receive His fullness by faith.
- We give over every area of our lives to Him, but this is only half the process. Once we have given our lives to Him entirely, then we want to receive His fullness entirely.

- Since He is utterly holy, prior to our receiving His fullness, we should plead the blood of the Lord Jesus Christ to cleanse us from all sin, telling Him we are willing to repent, renounce and make restitution for any sin He reveals.
- Plead the promise and believe that He has filled you.

Now, are you ready to genuinely pray, "Holy Spirit, fill me"? He will fill you to overflowing!

Rev. Fred Hartley, III, is Senior Pastor of the Lilburn Alliance Church, Lilburn, Georgia.

	Prayer for
CHAPTER	**Healing**
10	*by Joseph Arthur*

FOR CHRISTIANS TODAY "DIVINE HEALING" is a controversial term. Much of what is called divine healing is neither divine nor healing. Our prayers for the sick are often ineffective. We pray, and some get well and some die. We forget to pray, and people get well anyhow.

Many Christians do not know how to pray for the sick. When they pray ineffectively, their faith ultimately weakens.

I believe in divine healing! We in The Christian and Missionary Alliance believe that Jesus Christ is the great Physician. He does heal us! On the cross He bore our sins of the spirit, our physical ailments, our mental anguishes. On the cross He defeated Satan and his demonic forces. On the cross and by His resurrection He provided ultimate victory over death itself.

In his first letter to the Thessalonian believers,

Paul says: "May God himself, the God of peace, sanctify you through and through. May your whole spirit, soul and body be kept blameless at the coming of our Lord Jesus Christ. The one who calls you is faithful and he will do it" (5:23–24).

Holiness before Happiness

God's primary concern for us is not our happiness but our holiness. When Jesus heals us, it is so we are better equipped for ministry in His kingdom.

Sickness may strike in various ways affecting the whole person. Consequently, healing must occur in corresponding areas.

There is (1) healing of the spirit, referring to the spiritual sickness caused by sin; (2) healing from the effects of past hurts, popularly called "inner healing" or the "healing of damaged emotions"; (3) healing of the physical body, including illnesses that have damaged body tissue or disorders in which structures and organs malfunction; (4) healing from demonic activity within a person; and (5) healing of the dying, involving comfort and strength for those passing through the final ordeal of earthly existence.

Ask the Right Questions

Answers to prayer do not arrive automatically. True, God "is able to do immeasurably more than all we ask or imagine" (Ephesians 3:20), but it is "according to his power that is at work within us" and for the purpose of bringing "him . . . glory in the church and in Christ Jesus throughout all generations, for ever and ever!" (3:21).

In praying for divine healing within any of the above-mentioned five areas, it is necessary to ask three questions: (1) What is the basic sickness? (2) What is the basic cause? (3) What is the prayer? Each of the five kinds of sickness requires a specific kind of healing and a specific kind of prayer.

We ask the first question—What is the basic sickness?—in order to ascertain which of the five types of sickness we are confronting, whether sickness of the spirit, emotional hurt, physical distress, demonic activity or sickness unto death. Here is where the gift of discernment is important. Not always can we rely on circumstantial evidence or even the statement of the person seeking healing. But if we lack wisdom, God promises to supply it— if we believe and do not doubt (James 1:5–6).

We will briefly consider each type of sickness as we ask and answer questions two and three.

Healing of the Spirit

Exactly what do we mean by a sickness of the spirit? The Bible sees each human being as a trinity of spirit, soul and body. It speaks of the powerful word of God "piercing even to the dividing asunder of soul and spirit, and of the joints and marrow [the physical being]" (Hebrews 4:12, KJV). With our body we are best acquainted, having spent many hours before the mirror admiring it. The soul is the behavior mechanism that enables the body to calculate, to react, to decide. The soul is also a trinity—of mind, emotions and will. It is the seat of all creaturely behavior. Neither animals nor human beings need any particular relationship to God in order to behave.

But we humans differ from animals in that we have a spirit—something God has not given to any other form of created life. This God-created spirit within enables us to receive and be motivated by the very life of God Himself. It enables us to enjoy God and to be enjoyed by God. Sickness of the spirit hinders our functional relationship with God.

What Causes Sickness of Spirit?

What causes sickness of the spirit? What hinders us from functioning the way God intended? In his second letter to the Corinthian Christians, Paul counseled them to "purify [them]selves from everything that contaminates body and spirit, perfecting holiness out of reverence for God" (7:1). He was concerned about the health and purity of the Corinthians' lives, including their spirits.

Sickness of the spirit goes back to Genesis 3. The action begins with a spiritually healthy Adam and

Eve enjoying an open relationship with God and with each other. Enter the Tempter. And the transgression. *Enter sin.* Result? Sickness of the spirit. As with Adam and Eve, so with us: *The cause of sickness of the spirit is our own personal sin.*

Sin created guilt, and Adam and Eve hid from God. They became estranged from their Creator. They became self-centered instead of God-centered. They became sick in spirit.

What Kind of Prayer?

So what kind of prayer is needed for divine healing to occur? The first and deepest healing that Christ brings is the forgiveness of our sins. When there is sickness of the spirit, the only effective prayer is the prayer of repentance. Jesus, who died for our sins, will forgive us and bring healing provided we have a change of attitude and turn from our sin. This is healing at the deepest level. Often it will carry over to the healing of damaged emotions—even to physical healing.

Primarily we are spiritual beings. If the basic problem is with the spirit, the spirit must be dealt with first. Do you remember the paralytic mentioned in Mark 4? Do you remember Jesus' first words to him? " 'Son, your sins are forgiven' " (2:5). Jesus discerned the man's primary need to be healing of the spirit, due to sin. Then he addressed the man's physical paralysis.

I have discovered that people want to get their physical needs met without getting right with God spiritually. When someone comes forward to pray during one of our worship services, the first question our counseling team asks is, "Do you know of any unconfessed sin in your life?" If the answer is yes, a counselor suggests they pray first for forgiveness—spiritual healing. Only after that do we lay hands on the person and pray for healing of body. All prayer must lead to Calvary. We shortchange people if we pray to get them out of their circumstances and do not lead them to the cross, where they can find spiritual healing.

Healing of Damaged Emotions

One of the real problems in a ministry of healing is the tendency to oversimplify, to jump to conclusions. In 25 years as a minister both overseas and in North America, I have discovered that the ordinary ways of ministering will never help some problems. I had to develop a special "inner healing" prayer · ministry to help those with unhealed memories.

Somewhere between our personal sins and our physical ailments lies that part of our lives where we discover many of our real failings as human beings. If it is what we might term emotional sickness, what is its basic cause?

Usually emotional sickness is caused by emotional

hurts of our past. We can pray and repent, but we still bear the problem. I dealt with a mentally depressed woman who could not believe God loved her, because her whole life experience shouted that *no one* cared about her.

If Christ came to bring salvation and freedom, does He not include hope for people who have been badly wounded psychologically?

How to Pray

Emotional problems stem from several different causes. Paul found himself despairing because of physical hardships and pressures (2 Corinthians 1:8). Sometimes depression has a physical source; we should check for a hidden problem like this. A sinful response to life's experiences is also a common cause of emotional problems.

How do I pray for emotional sickness? The basic idea of inner healing is simply this: Jesus, who is the same yesterday, today and forever, can take the memories of our past and heal them from the remaining wounds, filling us with His love. But the wounds must first be drained of the poison of past hurts and resentments.

Inner healing is seldom accomplished in a one-time prayer session. Healing occurs gradually or progressively. But God *does* want to heal us from these hurts. We can ask Jesus Christ to walk back with us in time to when we were hurt and to free us from the present effects of that wound. This kind of praying involves two things: (1) bringing to light and discussing with another person what has hurt us, and (2) praying to God to heal the binding effects of the hurtful past incidents.

Physical Healing

Physical healing is perhaps hardest for us to believe for. Yet real physical healings do take place regularly. If the sickness is physical, our second question follows: "What is its cause?"

Some insist that all physical sickness is the result of unconfessed sin or a lack of faith. That is a half truth. There can be other reasons for physical sickness: for example, the violation of natural laws such as the necessity of a balanced diet and adequate exercise; old age; divine discipline. Sometimes physical sickness is for God's glory. Paul's "thorn" in his flesh was occasion for God to demonstrate His power (2 Corinthians 12:7–9).

A Personal Testimony

One morning I awoke with severe chest pains and electric-like sensations radiating down my arms. At the hospital they ruled out heart disease. But I noticed a developing paralysis down my left side. By evening I could not stand. After further tests, the neurologist made his diagnosis. I had had a severe attack of multiple-sclerosis that might well put me in a wheelchair for life.

After 40 days in the hospital, wondering how God could be glorified in those circumstances, I was listening as my wife, Donna, read Psalm 116 aloud. The Holy Spirit impressed on me four thoughts as she read. If I would (1) confess my sin and (2) always give God the glory, He would (3) save me from destruction and (4) keep my feet from stumbling. I promised compliance.

Over the next few days, I had the privilege of leading 39 nurses and 2 doctors to faith in Christ. And gradually physical healing came also. Today I am senior pastor of the C&MA Church in Santa Rosa, California.

How Do We Pray?

Some insist that modern medicine has no place in divine healing. In many cases this means missing out on a significant healing that can be provided by modern medical treatment. Some limit the way God heals *only* to modern medical treatment. This also is a mistake. Physical illness may be caused by spiritual and emotional—even demonic—influences. For healing to take place, total treatment is necessary.

How do we pray for physical healing? The key Scripture is James 5:13–18. These divinely inspired instructions, intended for the church age, have never been revoked. Note that God prescribes two groups of pray-ers: (1) The elders who have been called are to "pray over [the sick person] and anoint him with oil in the name of the Lord" (5:14). (2) The congregation and, by implication, the sick person are to confess their sins to each other and pray for each other so they may be healed (5:16).

For what do we pray? There are three prayers that we must be aware of as we determine what is appropriate. Since the person making the request is a believer, we must first be sure there is no sin in his or her life. He must search his heart. She must turn from all sin. Better to meet God in sickness than miss God in health.

The first prayer is one of thankfulness. God is disciplining a son or daughter whom He loves. The second prayer is one of repentance—the petitioner's response to God's corrective. The third prayer is one of comfort in affliction. When God does not heal at once, He gives something as valuable—His sustaining grace. Sometimes divine healing comes immediately, sometimes progressively, sometimes at glorification. But God always heals His people.

Healing for the Demonized

Some are sick because of demonic affliction. Jesus healed the demonized. The Scriptures, church tradition and human experience all testify to the existence of the devil and demons. Jesus' life and ministry was marked by continual confrontations with demons. He gave authority to His followers to cast out demons.

The Bible is clear about the believer's spiritual warfare: "Your enemy the devil prowls around like a roaring lion looking for someone to devour. Resist him, standing firm in the faith" (1 Peter 5:8–9). When it comes to spiritual warfare, every Christian needs to know that while Satan is strong, Christ is stronger!

Demons cannot own or have absolute control of Christians. But Christians who live in unconfessed sin can be affected by demons.

How do we pray for a person demonized? By a radically different focus. Prayer for healing is directed to God. Prayer for deliverance from demons is directed to the oppressing spirits. Prayer for healing is a petition. Prayer for deliverance is a command. We order them *in the name of Jesus Christ the Lord* to depart. Ideally, the exorcism of demons should be a team ministry, rather than a ministry done alone.

Christ has equipped us adequately for this battle (see Ephesians 6:10-18). As in other endeavors, we are to rely on God's strength and not our own.

The Problem of Death

After my 25 years of ministry, I can attest that death comes heavy handed. Where does divine healing figure as a heartbroken father or a devastated widow stands by a newly-filled grave?

Ultimately, original sin brought on death. In most cases, the more immediate cause has been physical disease or accident. The death that is ever resident in our bodies has become dominant, and physical life has ceased.

But life is not measured by the length of physical existence on earth. Human life does not cease at physical death. The inner being, comprised of spirit and soul, lives on. For the believer, that continued life is in heaven, where we are clothed in the holiness and glory of Christ.

What, then, is our prayer when death strikes a believer? First, we believe that Jesus died—an actual physical death that atoned for our sins (1 Corinthians 15:3). Second, we believe that Jesus rose from the dead, and in so doing, He broke the power of death and removed its sting (15:4, 55). Because He lives, we live. Third, we believe that Christians who have died will accompany Jesus when He returns to earth (1 Thessalonians 4:14). Fourth, we believe there will be a reuniting of physical body (albeit in imperishable form) with soul and spirit (1 Corinthians 15:42–44; 1 Thessalonians 4:16). In our reconstituted bodies our glory-clothed soul and spirit will be perfect forever in the presence of Christ.

Should We Pray for Healing?

If people who are dying are to be promoted through death into the unspeakable glories of heaven, we should not take it for granted that God wants to heal them here on earth. Our prayer might better be to encourage them about what lies ahead, and then provide comfort for those they leave behind.

When my mother received the diagnosis of inoperable cancer, her doctors suggested chemotherapy, even though they held out no hope of a cure. Mother, who had experienced divine physical healing many times before, believed it was now God's time to take her home. She was not afraid of death. Although she regretted leaving husband and family, she was looking forward to seeing Jesus and her family in heaven.

Mother's final days were ones of sweet communion with God and family. She prayed the prayer of faith that God would take her home, and she went joyously into the arms of Jesus. That, too, is divine healing.

Health is being at peace with God. For the Christian, the ultimate healing is death and resurrection and a glorified body! "There is a time for everything," said the Preacher— "a time to be born and a time to die" (Ecclesiastes 3:1–2). Release is as much a part of healing as physical restoration.

God Is the Healer

Whether through medicine or direct, God is the ultimate Healer. We may do the treating, but God does the curing. Our treatment, our tenderness can be very important, but we must remember always that God is the Healer.

Dr. Joe Arthur is the Senior Pastor of the Santa Rosa Alliance Church, Santa Rosa, California.

<table>
<tr><td>

CHAPTER

11

</td><td>

Prayer and the
Second Coming

by William R. Goetz
</td></tr>
</table>

CHAPTER

11

Prayer and the Second Coming

by William R. Goetz

TWO PEOPLE ON THE PLATFORM of a rural railroad station in the by-gone days of frequent rail travel awaited the arrival of a train.

One, the station agent—who knew the train schedules backwards and forwards—did so in a perfunctory fashion as part of his routine responsibility. No excitement or need for special preparation motivated him.

The other occupant of the platform was in a state of keen anticipation, eagerly peering down the track to catch the first glimpse of the expected train. Though she did not have much knowledge about the schedule or the railroad's workings, she knew that a train was due to arrive soon, and she could scarcely wait.

For, on that train was her beloved fiancé—coming for their long-awaited wedding day.

The eagerness of the bride-to-be certainly provides an excellent illustration of the attitude the earnest Christian should have in relationship to the second coming of the Lord Jesus Christ, and particularly in the matter of prayer.

Parousia

Jesus Christ is coming back to earth!

• The Old Testament writers frequently provided prophetic previews of this fact, just as they did concerning the First Advent.

• Our Lord Himself predicted and promised it—in His Olivet Discourse (recorded in Matthew 24, Mark 13 and Luke 21) and in His declaration during the Last Supper, when He said, "And if I go and prepare a place for you, I will come back and take you to be with me that you also may be where I am" (John 14:3).

• The two angels, at the time of His ascension into heaven, told the disciples, "This same Jesus, who has been taken from you into heaven, will come back in the same way you have seen him go into heaven" (Acts 1:11).

• The writers of the New Testament referred to the second coming of Jesus Christ again and again—over 300 times in total.

This "blessed hope" of the return of Jesus Christ to earth to rule and reign as King is a key aspect of the four-fold gospel.

What a wonderful fact is this prospect of the *parousia! Parousia* (Greek) means "presence" or "coming," as it is variously translated. It is the word most frequently used in the New Testament of our Lord's return and describes both the rapture and the revelation of Christ (1 Corinthians 15:23; 1 Thessalonians 4:15–18; Matthew 24; 1 Thessalonians 3:13; 2 Peter 1:16).

Arndt and Gingrich show that the word [parousia], found in classical writings and in the apocryphal books as well as in the New Testament, has developed in two directions. It is used by false cults to express the coming of a hidden divinity and, on the other hand, has become the official term for the visit of a person of high rank. In view of the latter, the use of parousia in connection with the Lord's return is fitting. When translated "presence" it means the presence made possible by the coming of the individual. (The Zondervan Pictorial Bible Dictionary, 1963, p. 623.)

And, though not everyone who holds this blessed hope agrees on the exact schedule of the Bridegroom's "train" (to borrow from our illustration above), there can be no question that His coming is near. Unfortunately, because of the frequently unwise and unbiblical tendencies of various prophecy buffs to set inaccurate dates for the rapture, the entire truth has become neglected—even shunned.

However, students of the prophetic Scriptures, though they may differ in their understanding of the exact chronology of the end-time events, cannot escape the conviction that the return is near.

There are at least six significant signs which support such a conviction.

1. The existence of the nation Israel

In His Olivet Discourse, Jesus gave the parable of the fig tree near the end of His major prophetic message about the end times and His return. He said that just as the appearance of leaves on the fig tree indicates that summer is near, so the appearance of the signs He had listed—against the backdrop of a regathered Israel—would indicate that He "was near, right at the door" (Matthew 24:32–33). He added that the generation that saw these events "will certainly not pass away until *all* these things have happened" (24:34).

Israel has been called "the fig tree nation." While not all believers accept this view, the clear references to this symbolism in Jeremiah 24:1–10 and in the encounter of Christ with the Jewish religious leaders (Matthew 24:32–33) as well as the references in Judges 9:10–11 and Luke 21:29–31 make a very good case for such a conviction. Dr. Walter Wilson in *This Means That* says, "The fig tree is usually a type of the nation Israel in its political aspect as the channel of God's blessing to the nations of earth" (Evangelical Publishers, 1943, p. 96).

There can be no question that the existence of the modern-day nation of Israel is miraculous. It is without precedent in the annals of human history that a people would be deprived of nationhood for 19 centuries, be scattered among the nations of earth and yet retain identity and become re-established, against incredible odds, in its former land.

That this occurred on May 14, 1948, followed by numerous remarkable preservations of that nation, as well as her occupation, since 1967, of Jerusalem, is viewed by many as the beginning (at the very least) of a major prophetic fulfillment.

2. The potential of an invasion of this regathered Israel

The prophet Ezekiel, in chapters 37–39, describes the regathering of Israel after her lengthy world-wide dispersal in his well-known "dry bones" prophecy. This is followed by a prophetic description of an invasion of this regathered Israel by a confederacy of nations led by a northern power, which many believe to be descriptive of Russia.

While recent events in the former Soviet Union have made it appear that the previously indicated communist animosity and threat to Israel is over, there are numerous reasons to seriously question such a conclusion.

In any event the conditions for the fulfillment of

Ezekiel's prophecy certainly exist—and indicate the nearness of end-time events.

3. The apparent foreshadowings of the final human empire foretold by Daniel

The "march of empires" prophetically described by Daniel in chapters 2 and 7, as he interpreted Nebuchadnezzar's dream and recounted his own vision, appears to be reaching its climax. Many students of prophecy believe that the rise of the European Common Market—which on January 1, 1993, became the "United States of Europe"—fits the picture as a definite foreshadowing of the 10-nation confederacy which will be in existence at the time the "God of heaven will set up a kingdom that will never be destroyed" (Daniel 2:44).

4. Preparations for the emergence of the prophesied Antichrist

A prophecy in John's Apocalypse (chapter 13) has occasioned a tremendous amount of speculation over the years, describing as it does the diabolical total control of the coming Antichrist. The idea that complete economic control could be achieved through the use of a mark, which is a number, has drawn skepticism and scorn for years.

Now, however, the advent of the computer, electronic fund transfers, the UPC, debit banking, the laser and numerous other technological advances has made such control a virtual reality. Thus, technologically, as well as politically (see number 3 above) and spiritually (see number 5 below), the stage is rapidly being set for the reign of the counterfeit Christ, who will strut upon earth's stage just prior to the revelation of Christ from heaven.

5. The rise of a prophesied global religion which complements the reign of the Antichrist

Chapter 17 of John's Apocalypse is understood by many to describe prophetically the counterfeit (prostitute) religion called "Mystery Babylon" which is part of the rise to power by the Antichrist. While various denominations have been made out to be candidates for this role, many students believe that no one church, but rather a system, fits the biblical picture. The New Age movement—global, pervasive and with its roots back in the Genesis 3 temptation by Satan—appears to be completely suited to the role. Its rise to prominence, out of all proportion to its size, is seen as an indicator of the nearness of earth's final human chapter.

6. The appearance of the "birth pain" signs which Jesus said would precede His Revelation

In the Olivet Discourse the Lord Jesus answered three questions from His disciples: (1) When would [the destruction of Herod's Temple] be? (2) What would be the sign of His coming? and (3) What would be the sign at the end of the age?

Jesus replied with a description of signs which He said would be like birth pains (Matthew 24:8). Thus, just as the pains of birth begin at a point in time and then increase in frequency and severity up to the moment of birth, so it would be with the indicators Jesus gave.

A summary of the discourse reveals signs like these:

> • *Wars,* and as part of that sign, rumors of wars, commotions, nation (Greek *ethnos*—racial) rising against nation and kingdom against kingdom.
> • *Great earthquakes* in various places.
> • *Famines.*
> • *Pestilences.*
> • Unusual, frightening *signs in the heavens,* including fearful sights, great signs from the heavens, signs in the sun, moon and stars, with the powers of heaven being shaken.
> • *Jerusalem restored to Jewish control* AFTER a worldwide dispersion and return to Israel by the Jews.
> • *Distress* of nations, *with perplexity.*
> • Men's fainting from *fear* at what is coming on the earth.
> • *False christs.*

> • A worldwide proclamation of the
> gospel.

The presence of such conditions in the world—against the backdrop of a regathered Israel in control of Jerusalem—leads to the conviction that the hour grows late.

Thus, regardless of the eschatalogical viewpoint one holds, it is apparent that the *parousia* is nearing. How should this affect the prayer life of the obedient earnest believer?

Petition

A careful survey of the Scriptures reveals that there is very little direct connection, textually, between the *parousia* and prayer.

In fact, unless the exhortation to "watch" is viewed as a directive to pray, as it sometimes is since it is frequently coupled with the exhortation to pray, there appear to be only two or three verses which contain a *direct* connection between the two.

One of these, and undoubtedly the best known, is the final recorded prayer of the Bible in Revelation 22:20. Here the Apostle John, by inspiration, responds to the statement of the Lord Jesus Christ that He is coming quickly by praying, "Amen. Come, Lord Jesus" (Revelation 22:20). Such a petition has been frequently reiterated by believers throughout the centuries.

A second direct connection is to be found in what

we call The Lord's Prayer. Here Jesus taught believers that we are to pray, "Your kingdom come" (Matthew 6:10). While there is certainly the sense in which Christ's spiritual kingship can be realized in individual lives, this petition undoubtedly has as its focus the literal reign of Christ.

The apostle Paul's prayers for the church at Thessalonica, recorded in 1 Thessalonians 3:11–13 and 5:23, contain a definite connection to the *parousia,* for the apostle prays that God will work in the lives of believers to achieve certain spiritual disciplines and goals in the light of His return. He prays that love for one another and all men will increase and overflow, that they may be blameless and holy at the coming of the Lord Jesus Christ.

Apart from these references, however, no direct connection is to be found in Scripture.

Principle

But, while very few *direct* scriptural second coming/prayer connections exist, this does not mean that there isn't a major relationship between the two.

The principles of the Christian life clearly call for such a connection.

In the matter of prayer these principles are clear:

• Prayer is *commanded* for the believer.
• Prayer is *characteristic* of the believer.
• Prayer is *crucial* to the believer.

Prayer is commanded. The word "command" is not too strong a term to use in describing the language of Scripture. True, we as believers are graciously *invited* to come boldly to the throne, as children to a Father/King, but we are also citizens and soldiers, and our Sovereign/Commander *directs* us to pray. This is made clear by action verbs like "seek," "ask," "knock" and specific directions such as "pray continually," "in everything by prayer . . ." as well as the teaching of Jesus (such as the parable in Luke 18 to show His disciples that they should *always* pray).

Prayer is characteristic. The words of the hymn writer: "Prayer is the Christian's vital breath, / the Christian's native air" are amply demonstrated in the life of the Lord Jesus Christ, as well as in the lives of godly believers through the centuries. One of the things that happens in the life of a person who is truly born again and growing spiritually is that he *wants* to pray—and he does pray.

Prayer is crucial. The classic portion on the warfare of the saints—Ephesians 6:10–18—concludes with the urgent directive to "pray in the Spirit on all occasions with all kinds of prayers and requests. With this in mind, be alert and always keep on praying for all the saints." This word, in the context of the Christian's armor and warfare, clearly underscores the crucial nature of persistent, Spirit-led prayer.

As someone has well said, "When we simply work we get what *man* can do. When we pray we get what *God* can do."

Now, since prayer is indeed commanded, characteristic and crucial, and therefore unquestionably a significant part of the life of every obedient Spirit-filled believer, it is only logical to conclude that its importance would be heightened by the prospect of the return of Christ.

If the whole tenor of the Scripture on the return urges anything, it urges faithfulness on the part of God's children in the light of the Second Coming of Christ.

Therefore—among other responses—PRAY!!

Practice

The truth of the second coming is given to Christians as a blessed hope to stimulate spiritual life. It is intended to have a moral, ethical and spiritual effect in the lives of believers, as Titus 2:11–14 makes clear.

If this blessed hope is truly believed and honestly held, it will be a strong motivation to prayer. If I am really convinced that the coming of the Lord is imminent, I will commit myself to communion with Him on behalf of my own needs, as well as the needs of my family, my church, the lost, our nation and the missionary enterprise.

• **Prayer for personal holiness.** First John 3:3 indicates that "every man who has [the hope of Christ's return] in him purifies himself, just as He is pure." Prayer will undoubtedly be a part of such spiritual discipline.

• Prayer for family needs. An earnest desire that every member of one's immediate and extended family be ready for the Lord's return—through salvation and spiritual growth—is a strong motivation to prayer.

• Prayer for the lost. Perhaps some of those who are yet lost are family members. Others may be friends, neighbors or associates. A genuine concern for the eternal destiny of these people, coupled with a desire to obey the Lord and an awareness of His soon return, should powerfully stir us to persistent prayer.

• Prayer for the church and our nation. We ought to faithfully uphold in prayer those in authority. This certainly includes all who provide leadership within our local fellowships and in our wider denominational circles. It definitely means to also pray for government leaders—"for kings and all those in authority" (1 Timothy 2:2).

• Prayer for the missionary enterprise. The earnest desire of Albert B. Simpson over 100 years ago to see the gospel proclaimed to every nation and so to "bring back the King" was what has been called "the engine that powered the early Alliance missionary thrust." Can any who follow in that train fail to pray earnestly for the missionary messengers—in the light of our being so much nearer to His appearing?

In recent years I have had frequent opportunity to preach in numerous churches. A disturbing fact has come to my attention. It is the extreme rarity that congregations (even Alliance congregations) are led in public prayer for missionaries and/or government leaders. The unwelcome thought persists that, if such petitions are never uttered in public worship, they are probably seldom voiced in private prayer. How tragic!

The imminent return should motivate these and other earnest requests, as indicated above. Perhaps a loss of the sense and expectation of the return is part of the reason for a decline in prayerfulness in our lives and churches today.

How much better to embrace this great motivational truth, and in personal practice, pray daily in the spirit, if not the words, of that great Christian and Bible commentator of another era, Matthew Henry:

Even so, come, Lord Jesus; make haste, my beloved, and be thou like a roe, or like a young hart on the mountains of spices. Thus beats the pulse of the church, thus breathes that gracious Spirit which actuates and informs the mystical body of Christ; and we should never be satisfied till we find such a spirit breathing in us, and causing us to *look for the blessed hope, and glorious appearance of the great God and our Savior Jesus Christ. . . . Come, Lord Jesus,* put an end to this state of sin, sorrow and temptation; gather thy people out of this present evil world, and take them up to heaven, that state of perfect purity, peace, and joy, and so finish thy great design, and fulfil all that word in which thou hast caused thy people to hope.

Dr. William R. Goetz is the Senior Pastor of the Hillsdale Alliance Church in Regina, Saskatchewan.

Special
Prayers

Who may ascend the hill of the LORD?
Who may stand in his holy place?
He who has clean hands and a pure heart,
who does not lift up his soul to an idol
or swear by what is false.
(Psalm 24:3–4)

Create in me a pure heart, O God,
and renew a steadfast spirit within me.
Do not cast me from your presence
or take your Holy Spirit from me.
Restore to me the joy of your salvation
and grant me a willing spirit, to sustain me.
Then I will teach transgressors your ways,
and sinners will turn back to you.
(Psalm 51:10–13)

If I had cherished sin in my heart,
the Lord would not have listened.
(Psalm 66:18)

Warfare Prayer

by David P. Jones

THE 10 LONGEST DAYS IN the Christian era may have been the period between Jesus' ascension and the descent of the Holy Spirit at Pentecost. The 120 loyal followers of the Messiah, gathered in that second-floor Jerusalem meeting room, were "joined together constantly in prayer" (Acts 1:14).

And what was the object of their intercession? The power of the indwelling Holy Spirit—power to boldly witness to Jesus' death and resurrection in "Jerusalem . . . and to the ends of the earth" (1:8). They were about to face an implacable foe: Satan and his demonic hordes. Jesus' followers were about to begin the dismantling of Satan's empire.

A month and a half earlier, Christ had conclusively triumphed over Satan. His sinless life, His sacrificial death that fully satisfied God's absolute justice, His victorious resurrection from the dead left Satan a defeated adversary. But the bogus prince, the lying lord of the earth, was not about to give up. If he could just convince the infant Church that it was weak and ineffective, Christ's death blow to his counter-kingdom might never become known.

So for 10 days the followers of Jesus stayed and prayed; they persevered and prepared for war. In the close confines of that upper room, the disciples discovered that Christ's army marches on its knees. Warfare praying became the trademark of the apostolic church.

Christ Is Sovereign over Satan

Warfare prayer is not clamoring for future victory over Satan. It is proclaiming Christ's past-perfect victory at the cross and the empty tomb; it is administering Christ's present sovereignty over a defeated foe and his miserable minions.

As I preached in a simple plywood chapel in a poor Brazilian neighborhood, my theme that night was Christ the Sanctifier. It was the second night of our "Fourfold Gospel Campaign," and the little building was well filled with sincere believers who wanted to know more about the Holy Spirit and how He could fill them with His presence and power. Just as I was nearing the climax of my message, I saw the side door of the building open and a man poorly dressed and obviously drunk staggered through the doorway. Seeing me at the pulpit, he turned in my direction and shouted in perfect English, "I know who you are and I know where you came from!"

Without a moment's hesitation, I faced the intruder, pointed my hand toward the door and said, "In Jesus' name I command you: Get out!" Bang! The door shut and he was gone. The whole dialogue could not have taken more than 15 seconds.

I returned to my sermon, and within a few moments it was as if nothing had happened. At my invitation, a number of people came forward to seek the infilling of the Holy Spirit.

"Did He Say What I Heard Him Say?"

Afterward, my wife, Judy, questioned me: "Did that man really say what I heard him say?" She, too, had heard his remark in English and understood the words. The Portuguese-speaking church pastor, who recognized the man, also heard him speak but did not know what he was saying.

"Can that man speak English?" I asked the pastor.

"No," he replied. "He can hardly speak Portuguese right. He's the neighborhood drunk. He has come here to the chapel many times, but never before has he caused a problem."

The next day, the pastor saw the man at the local store and asked him about the previous night.

"It's a funny thing, pastor," the man began. "I was at the bar drinking and maybe had a few more drinks than I should have when I felt this compelling urge to go to church. When I opened that door,

I really don't know what happened. But that *gringo* at the pulpit sure got upset!" He assured the pastor that he did not speak English.

When the pastor reported this conversation to me, I understood fully what was behind the bizarre incident. This poor man, under Satan's bondage, had been compelled by demons to disrupt a church meeting in which I was explaining the Spirit's power to enable believers to witness to Christ's victory over Satan and thus participate in the establishment of God's kingdom. Naturally, that went against Satan's desires, so he tried to interfere. But he had not counted on the fact that the Holy Spirit was in control of the service and, thankfully, the preacher.

Discouraged Missionaries

A group of tired and rather discouraged missionaries had gathered at Hallelujah Valley Camp just outside Curitiba for one of our first-ever work retreats. All of us were feeling the pressures of the Lord's work. Some faced serious health problems. Some had children who struggled against difficulties in school. Our church-planting efforts were being met with resistance on every front. Lack of response and sky-high rent had forced us to abandon our two-year-old effort to establish a church in southern Brazil's Porto Alegre. Some of the Curitiba churches faced problems with their pastors.

More than half of all Brazilians are involved in the occult and demonic practices. The varied forms of spiritism have permeated all of Brazilian society, from the rich and powerful to the very poorest. Every effort to preach the gospel or plant the church of Christ is a difficult struggle.

As missionaries, we had come to Brazil with good training, good methodology and ideas, and what we had thought was boundless energy. Soon, however, we encountered the enemy face-to-face. We saw demonic manifestations in our churches and in the homes we visited. At the time, most of us had little or no training in spiritual warfare. We knew that Satan and a plethora of demons existed, that they were bad and that they fought against the work of God. But we did not comprehend just how powerful Satan's kingdom was or how we were to resist him and combat his demons.

Worst of all, we did not realize the primacy of prayer as our key to victory.

Important Counsel

David K. Volstad, our regional director, was with us at the retreat. We went over our work reports with him—reports that tended to be disheartening. We reviewed with him various strategies for ministry. But it was in one of his devotional messages that David Volstad passed on to us a simple yet powerful principle of the Christian life. It impacted all of us. We saw in it the reason for our weariness, our lack of success in ministry and the key to turning failure into victory.

"If we had prayed more, we would have worked less." The words were from Andrew Murray, but they were based solidly in the scriptures. "If we had prayed more, we would have worked less." Those few, short words were powerful—and so true! Only as we prayed, "Your kingdom come, / your will be done on earth as it is in heaven," could we expect to see God's work prosper in Brazil.

We returned to our places of ministry much encouraged. As we marched on our knees we could surmount the enemy's defenses.

The Believer "Commands" Satan

Warfare prayer takes a strong stance against Satan. The believer is exercising authority over the enemy. But the Christian soldier does not pray to the enemy. Rather he or she *commands* the enemy in the name of Jesus Christ. Paul's encounter with the young fortune teller in Philippi is a case in point.

The young woman followed Paul and his team, "shouting, 'These men are servants of the Most High God, who are telling you the way to be saved' " (Acts 16:17). Obviously, she did not do this because she was a booster of the gospel. But the fortune-telling demon within her wanted to confuse the people of Philippi into thinking that Paul and she were serving the same purpose—perhaps declaring essentially the same gospel.

Satan's tactics have not changed appreciably since then. He would still have us believe that all religions lead to the same goal. He is a liar and the father of liars and opposed to the redemption that God has uniquely provided through Jesus Christ. The prayer warrior must be so attuned to God's voice and message that he or she can immediately perceive the enemy's tactics and deal with them decisively.

The Apostles Practiced Warfare Prayer

The Book of Acts is replete with examples of warfare praying. The coming of the Holy Spirit in power at Pentecost drove those in the upper room to the streets, where they declared "the wonders of God" in more than a dozen languages (2:8–11). Peter's powerful sermon resulted in multitudes being "cut to the heart" with conviction; that day some 3,000 people were baptized and added to the church (2:37, 41).

Peter's powerful sermon did not come from a Saturday seminar on persuasive preaching. It came out of 10 days in the trenches of warfare praying. And throughout that post-Pentecost time, the believers "devoted themselves to the apostles' teaching and to the fellowship, to the breaking of bread and to prayer" (2:42). Did you see it? *"And to prayer."* Prayer was the secret of the Church's power and boldness.

Peter and John gave the crippled beggar heaven's better coin when they raised him up, perfectly healed, in Jesus' name (3:1–8). And when the miracle and the apostles' preaching riled the temple rulers to the point of jailing Peter and John and forbidding them to "speak or teach at all in the name of Jesus," the two men upon their release "went back to their own people and . . . they raised their voices together in prayer to God" (4:1, 3, 18, 23–24). It was warfare praying at its best (4:24–30). "After they prayed, the place where they were meeting was shaken. And they were all filled with the Holy Spirit and spoke the word of God boldly" (4:31). Warfare prayer is declaring the victory of Christ's kingdom and exercising His authority over Satan's rebel reign.

A New Year's Eve in Brazil

On New Year's Eve, 1992, I was walking the darkened beach of Santa Catarina Island. My wife and I had gone there right after Christmas (Brazil's summer) for a few days of sun, surf and rest. Now, late on this New Year's Eve, I was alone on the deserted beach, reminiscing upon the year that was fast closing.

As I strolled along the sand, I came upon a circle

of candles within which some carefully arranged white roses surrounded a few cigars and trinkets. I recognized it at once as a *despacho,* an offering to the spirits. On New Year's Eve literally millions of Brazilians from all over the nation go to the beaches to bring their offerings to "Iemanjá," the goddess of the sea. Dressing in white, the people light candles and offer flowers, perfume, liquor and other gifts. In return, they ask Iemanjá and all the other spirits they worship for their blessing and protection throughout the ensuing year.

As I continued my walk, I saw people beginning to arrive at the water's edge. My heart was saddened. "God," I prayed, "don't permit these lying, demonic spirits to receive worship and honor that is only due You. This is all of Satan and only leads to further involvement and delusion. Don't permit this celebration to take place here tonight. Bring a great rain. Drown the flames of the candles and drive these worshipers back to their homes and hotels." As I walked, I did battle against the enemy. I knew that other Christians throughout Brazil were also engaged in this battle.

A Revolting Scene

I observed for a few minutes as the leader of one group of spiritists carefully arranged dozens of candles, placing them in an intricate pattern, then lit them, sprinkling liquor over the whole arrangement and spreading flowers at the worship site. One of his white-clad helpers came dripping up from the ocean where he had just made a special offering to Iemanjá. The group of people waited expectantly for one of their number to begin to "manifest" a spirit. I knew that when it happened, the person would come under total demonic control, beginning to dance and whirl like a dervish at a fantastic pace. All was set for a Satanic "festa."

As I walked on, sickened and disgusted at what was taking place, I continued to pray in the Spirit. Audibly I rebuked Satan, "binding" him in Jesus' name. It was after 11 when I returned to the apartment where Judy and I were staying. I was still asking God to defeat Satan and to put to shame this godless worship.

Within just a few minutes the wind picked up, the sky clouded over and rain began to fall. How it rained! Soon the rain was coming down in sheets, whipped by gusting winds. The rain and wind extinguished all the candles along the beach and sent the worshippers scuttling for protection. The wind and wind-whipped waves made quick work of the elaborate offerings to Iemanjá. As I took my place with Christ in the heavenlies in warfare praying, Satan was indeed put to shame.

The Whole Armor

No treatment of warfare prayer can be complete

without reference to Paul's classic teaching on the subject in Ephesians 6:10-20. In that much-read passage, Paul begins by identifying and locating our spirit opponents in this continuing battle (6:12). Then he details our necessary armor: the belt of truth, the breastplate of righteousness, shoes of readiness to march for the gospel of peace, the shield of faith and the helmet of salvation—essentially defensive pieces. Finally, Paul unsheathes the sword of the Spirit, God's Word, the believer's offensive weapon in spiritual warfare (6:14–17).

We tend to overlook or ignore the last of these verses dealing with the Christian soldier's "full armor." Verse 18 links the success of combat against Satan and his hosts with such words as *prayer, petition, praying in the Spirit.* Just as soldiers in the field need some means of communication with their commanders, so the Christian needs orders from his headquarters in order to combat the enemy.

The speedy runners of ancient days have given way to high-tech communications and "sky spy" satellite links, but information between commander and troops remains essential to victory. In spiritual warfare, communication is of the highest strategic importance, because our Commander not only plots the objectives but fights the battles.

A Bad Year

The year 1980 was a bad one for me and my family in Brazil. I was busier than any person should be. I was field director, a church pastor and a teacher at our Bible Institute. Two of our three sons experienced near fatalities that year. Difficulties with rent contracts necessitated three moves. We had two car accidents—neither of them our fault. To make matters worse, we were robbed five times: twice in our house, once on the street, once at the Bible Institute and once (of all places) in the bank! To make matters still worse, Judy began to lose weight at an alarming rate. Doctors could not discover the problem.

One night as I returned from teaching, I shared with a local pastor the pressures my family and I were under, the battle fatigue we were feeling and the desperate sense of almost not being able to cope any longer. Together we wept and prayed, and my colleague interceded for me, claiming victory and deliverance from these satanic attacks.

It was at that time that God began to teach Judy and me one of His great truths: "My grace is sufficient for you" (2 Corintians 12:9). As we went over that truth, we came to see that we could go through this time of testing by His grace and power.

From that time on, my wife and I began the day by first of all praying. "Lord," we would say to God, "this is a new day. We ask You for strength for this day. Give us grace and peace and faith to live just today for You."

Our Deliverance Begins

As we sought God morning after morning, He began to bring to our minds the picture of a deep well of cool, refreshing water. God seemed to be saying, "That well is the limitless source of My grace. You will find it sufficient for your daily needs. Take your little dipper to that deep well and reach in. Draw enough water for the day at hand."

Deliverance was neither instantaneous nor permanent. But Judy and I began to live by faith. We went to the "well" daily to draw our needed supply of God's grace. Through prayer God taught us that we would have some difficult battle campaigns, but we could be victorious and come through intact as we would recognize our own weaknesses and His unsurpassing strength and grace.

Warfare prayer was the key to God's limitless well of grace.

When on the battle line against Satan and his hordes, we often can't see his moves or understand his strategies, but our General stands above the battle seeing all. As we pray, we are in instant contact with our Victorious Lord, who gives us victory.

Warfare prayer, according to Paul, has three functions: (1) it keeps us on battle alert for all the saints all over the field, (2) it brings the "words" that enable God's messengers to communicate the gospel effectively and (3) it encourages those communicators to speak and act "fearlessly" (Ephesians 6:18–19).

One of the ultimate purposes of spiritual warfare and warfare prayer is the evangelization of the lost. Warfare praying gives us the power to do heaven's work here on earth.

Rev. David Jones is an Alliance missionary and director of the Alliance Bible Institute in Sao Paulo, Brazil.

CHAPTER	Praying for
13	Workers

by Rexford A. Boda

"THE HARVEST IS PLENTIFUL BUT the workers are few. Ask the Lord of the harvest, therefore, to send out workers into his harvest field" (Matthew 9:37–38).

The setting for this significant quote from the Lord Jesus, recorded by both Matthew and Luke, came subsequent to the appointment of the 72 and prior to the commissioning of the 12. It was prompted as Jesus ministered to the needs of the people in the towns and villages through His teaching and preaching and in a most graphic way through His miracles of healing.

Jesus found the multitudes harassed and helpless, like sheep without a shepherd and He took compassion on them. It was plain that these people represented a harvest of overwhelming proportions which urgently required recruits. The need was great. Volunteers were needed. But the Lord did not first send runners to the nearest city to open a recruiting office. The first step is to pray to the Lord of the harvest to send out workers.

Praying: Recognizing God's Sovereignty

In voicing this command to His disciples, Jesus is underlining the sovereignty of God in all the successful operations of the church. This is an important reminder for a people who often have great confidence in their own abilities and commitment. Perhaps Peter is the most obvious example of such presumption. Noble in character, determined in will, as Jesus' darkest hour was approaching with rumors of betrayal and death disturbing their fellowship, Peter with utmost sincerity and confidence spoke out, "Even if all fall away on account of you, I never will." Despite the fact that he was one of the last to forsake Jesus, fear overtook him at the trial and he denied the Lord. For the rest of his life he remembered the lesson that our strength, our confidence and our calling is only adequate as it comes from God. We do not call ourselves, or send ourselves, but look to God the Father, the Lord of the harvest, for our calling.

Isaiah describes this in a most effective fashion in his sixth chapter.

"Woe to me!" I cried. "I am ruined! For I am a man of unclean lips, and I live among a people of unclean lips, and my eyes have seen the King, the Lord Almighty."

Then one of the seraphs flew to me with a live coal in his hand, which he had taken with tongs from the altar. With it he touched my mouth and said, "See, this has touched your lips; your guilt is taken away and your sin atoned for."

Then I heard the voice of the Lord saying, "Whom shall I send? And who will go for us?"

And I said, "Here am I. Send me!"

Matthew Henry captured a biblical truth when he noted that commissions given in answer to prayer are most likely to succeed.

Throughout the Scriptures there are examples of and exhortations to prayer which lay down some basic principles to the role and function of prayer. Prayer is a central and essential ingredient in the Christian life and most particularly to a successful Christian ministry. Its absence or infrequency leads to a life of spiritual impotence and a church fellowship with little impact on the community or the nation.

Immediately prior to the hour of His betrayal and to His death and suffering on the cross, Jesus recognized the only hope for His followers to carry out His plan for the nations was through the authority which came from the Father, the protection of the Father and the sanctifying work of His word and truth.

In His high priestly prayer in John 17, we see a

beautiful meshing of our dependence on a sovereign God with a dynamic, active life of faith. Jesus had been exemplary in carrying out His assignment. He prays to the Father, "I have brought you glory by completing the work you gave me to do." There is nothing here about a passive, inactive faith which waits on God to work without means. In perfect obedience, Jesus came to carry out the mandate established in the eternal council of the triune God. He was at the threshold of the awful, final step in His assignment. Over the years of His life He had been diligent in doing the work of His Father's house. He had felt the press of the crowd and had spent exhausting hours ministering to its needs.

Despite the demands of His ministry, we note the record of His extensive prayer life in words such as "he went up into a mountain to pray" (Luke 9:28) or "very early in the morning Jesus went off to a solitary place where he prayed" (Mark 1:35).

Now once again in a crucial hour of ministry, Jesus looks toward heaven and prays. He recites what has been accomplished on earth to the glory of the Father. He reviews the wonderful privileges of those who have accepted His message. "All I have is yours, and all you have is mine." He intercedes for them that they may have a full measure of joy and that they may be protected from the evil one.

Further, He prays for those who will respond to the message the followers of Christ will preach. He prays for the unity of God's people which demonstrates in a most effective fashion the great love of God, a message which draws all peoples to Himself.

Somehow, we need to be convinced of the strategic necessity of prayer. The Scriptures are most clear in instruction and example. When we come to the end of ourselves and there seemingly is no place to turn, we go to prayer recognizing that God is our only hope, His power is our only enabling, His guidance is our only wisdom and His plan is our only assurance of salvation and success. In times of spiritual coldness among God's people and moral decay in society, the road to revival and renewed spiritual vigor begins with prayer. Through this channel we return to our proper starting place, the Sovereign Lord in whom alone "we are more than conquerors."

Praying: Recognizing Our Inadequacy

We now turn to the corollary of the truth and reality of God's power and sovereignty. What we have already considered is an affirmation that our pilgrimage is one of living faith. All of this emphasizes that salvation and the Christian life are totally of grace. The beloved apostle makes this plain in John 15 using the analogy of the vine and the branches.

"I am the true vine and my Father is the gardener . . ."

"You are already clean because of the word I have spoken to you . . ."

"I am the vine; you are the branches. If a man remains in me and I in him, he will bear much fruit; apart from me you can do nothing. If anyone does not remain in me, he is like a branch that is thrown away and withers; such branches are picked up, thrown into the fire and burned. If you remain in me and my words remain in you, ask whatever you wish, and it will be given you. This is to my Father's glory, that you bear much fruit, showing yourselves to be my disciples . . ."

"You did not choose me, but I chose you and appointed you to go and bear fruit—fruit that will last. Then the Father will give you whatever you ask in my name. This is my command: Love each other."

Christ alone is the vine which gives us life, sustains us and enables us to bear fruit. It is through Christ that we are connected to the Sovereign God. Outside of Christ we are totally inadequate for the task. Jesus makes it forcefully clear in John 15 with these words, "apart from me you can do nothing." No more complete verdict could be given to the inadequacy of raw human effort. It does not even allow for partial success in bearing spiritual fruit.

The problem of our inadequacy is two-fold. We are by nature created and finite beings in the image of God. Secondly, through the trespass of one man sin entered the world and all mankind became sinners.

If the fall had not occurred, we still would have been inadequate in and of ourselves to do the work God calls us to do. Our finiteness, even before sin, called for us to be in a living relationship with the Creator God. Adam and Eve experienced just such a relationship as they communed with God in the garden. All they had they received from their Creator—their life, their intelligence, their ability to fellowship and commune with Him and the whole realm of nature. Man's total inability to function independently and detached from God is captured well by Paul when he pointed out to the skeptics of the Areopagus this truth, "For in him we live and move and have our being."

When sin came through mankind's disobedience, a gulf of sin separated us from our fellowship with a holy God. The image of God by which we functioned was seriously marred and warped as we lost our original righteousness, holiness and clear knowledge of God. Previously, man would have been inadequate, even in his innocence, if he had not had a living relationship with God. Now, he is totally and hopelessly inadequate having been separated from God because of his sin.

Praying: Asking God to Send Workers

"Ask the Lord of the harvest, therefore, to send out workers into his harvest field." There is an urgency to this command born out of Christ's compassion for the multitude. His shepherd heart takes this occasion to impress upon His disciples the immensity of the task and the part they can play in meeting the need.

The emphasis here is on sending, with the connotation of action and thrusting forth. There is a connection here with the concept of being called. The candidates for being sent have been called. The idea of calling is being called to someone or to some task. We speak of calling on the name of the Lord, or somehow coming into a relationship with the Lord, of drawing near to the Lord for purposes of help and salvation. Paul often uses the term to speak of his calling to be an apostle, called by God for the purpose of being set apart for the gospel of God.

The emphasis of calling is a *calling to*. In our context, the concept of sending is a thrusting out in a most practical and dynamic way. It is a sending to bring men and women to Christ through the means of the one being sent out. The beginning of that process is praying to the Lord of the harvest that He will thrust forth workers.

It is abundantly clear that God has chosen to accomplish His will in the world and to administer His program of redemption through His servants in the flesh. Obviously, with a lone exception, He could have done His work through an immediate act of His divine power or through the mediation of angelic beings. However, throughout redemptive history, over and over again the Lord makes Himself known to mankind through His chosen servants. He chooses individuals to be agents and channels for His redemptive work. He sends His heralds to proclaim the message of the gospel to sinners who are dead in the transgressions and sins in which they live.

The one exception to the possibility that God could have accomplished His purposes without the agency of mankind and the one opposite exception that He could carry out His plan solely by the agency of mankind is the work of the God-man, Christ Jesus. He was first Immanuel, God with us, who alone could accomplish this task and who was to be declared with power to be the Son of God by His resurrection from the dead. He was also, of necessity, a descendant of David, the second Adam, the seed of the woman, man himself who paid the debt of sin and purchased our salvation once and for all. To say it again, God sent His Son, the second person of the triune God-head, to pay man's penalty for sin. This was possible because the Word became flesh, the Son came in the likeness of sinful man to be a sin offering, and so He condemned sin in sinful man.

So now, mankind through Christ is restored to an open and loving relationship with God because sin no longer separates him. Justified by faith he has peace with God. He is now able to receive the fullness and power of the Holy Spirit which will enable him to be an effective witness and worker in the harvest.

Seeing that Jesus has made it clear that we are to petition the Lord of the harvest to send forth workers, we have an awesome responsibility in the day in which we live. The plight of the crowds and multitudes is still enough to stir the compassion of Christ and of those who follow Him. Although the Lord of the harvest is blessing and bringing millions to Himself each year in many areas of the world, the forces of hedonism, materialism, secular humanism, the occult and multiplied other non-redemptive religions aggressively promote their own world views and lifestyles. They resist the unique claims of Christ and represent a massive harvest of souls who in their darkness and confusion are harassed and helpless, like sheep without a shepherd.

It is incumbent on us to pray in obedience to the instruction of Christ's command. Let us pray recognizing that it is God's work to send forth laborers. Paul expresses it this way in Ephesians 4:8 and 11.

"When he ascended on high he led captives in his train and gave gifts to men."

"It was he who gave some to be apostles, some to be prophets, some to be evangelists, and some to be pastors and teachers."

Let us pray recognizing that often those who prayed were also sent, exactly as happened when Jesus sent out the 12 after the commanded prayer was exercised.

Praying: Asking God for a Heart Willing to Send Workers

It is clear that as we come to the close of the 20th century, the work of the gospel will require a groundswell in the number of new workers for the harvest, whether it be the traditional roles of ministry or those working in effective lay ministries. This will be a challenge because, especially in the western world, our sense of sacrifice and commitment to the Lord's work has been dulled by the inroads of materialism, pleasure and a desire for security. We all too frequently guard our own interests.

Two passages of Scripture serve as a paradigm for not only praying that the Lord of the harvest will send forth workers, but also that we will be willing to let them go if they are called.

Acts 13:1–3 records the story of Barnabas and

Saul being set apart for their missionary labors. The setting was Antioch and the text gives evidence of a successful church. No doubt the leaders of the church were hard pressed to keep up with the demands of ministry. In the midst of it all, while worshiping, fasting and praying, the Holy Spirit in unmistakable terms made it clear that Barnabas and Saul were to be commissioned for ministry elsewhere. One can imagine some hesitancy in releasing two of their most gifted workers at a time when they needed all the help they could get. But the writer indicates that "after they had fasted and prayed, they placed their hands on them and sent them off."

Should God lay His hand on one of our gifted leaders or even on one of our key young people, would we be as quick to respond to the direction of the Lord and release them with our blessing and encouragement? This is a question for frequent asking in our local churches.

This is also a most appropriate question when it comes to our families. The Scriptures are full of examples where a commitment to harvest ministry was a rich family tradition. One thinks of Peter and Andrew, and of James and John, as well as the family of Jesus including James and Jude, and John the Baptist.

In First Samuel 1, we find a most striking example of a family commitment to the work of God. Hannah was barren, and although she enjoyed the love of her husband, she longed for a child. So she prayed for a son and promised to give him to the Lord for His service. God honored her prayer and she was faithful to her vow saying, "I will give him to the Lord. For his whole life he will be given over to the Lord." No doubt she hesitated in giving up the longed-for son at such a young age. But the Lord had a greater joy for her as he became the great judge of Israel.

Those of us who are parents today need to be careful that our desire to want what's best for our children does not fall into the trap of striving for security at the expense of not heeding the calling of the Lord.

The hymn "O Zion Haste" captures the essence of a heart praying for the work of the kingdom and for workers for the harvest.

> O Zion haste, thy mission high fulfilling
>   To tell to all the world that God is light,
> That he who made all nations is not willing
>   One soul should perish, lost in shades of night.
> Give of thy sons to bear the message glorious;
>   Give of thy wealth to speed them on their way;
> Pour out thy soul for them in prayer victorious;
>   And all thou spendest Jesus will repay.

We see in these words only a positive response to

the Great Commission—"Therefore, go and make disciples of all nations." There is no careful guarding of family and wealth with an unbalanced emphasis on a security which all too easily vanishes into a vapor. There is no evidence of guarding our time and resources so that we may labor tearing down barns and building bigger ones. In contrast, this hymn captures the message of Scripture which teaches that whatever we spend on the work of the kingdom will bring manifold dividends in this present age and in the age to come eternal life. "And all thou spendest, Jesus will repay."

In praying for workers, we need to pray for one another. We need to pray that God will work in our hearts making us willing to go. We need to pray for a willingness to let friends and associates go as God leads. For many of today's parents especially, we need to pray for a heart open to the will of God, capable of letting our children go with the freedom to follow God's call.

Finally, even as we have prayed that the Lord of harvest would send forth workers, we need to pray for those workers. The great leaders and heroes in the history of redemption were men and women of prayer, from Abraham through Paul. The many writings of Paul demonstrate that he was not only instrumental in sending workers out, but he was also faithful and constant in his prayer support. To the Philippians he writes words of comfort and assurance:

"I thank my God every time I remember you. In all my prayers for all of you, I always pray with joy because of your partnership in the gospel from the first day until now, being confident of this, that he who began a good work in you will carry it on to completion until the day of Christ Jesus."

May we ever be so faithful in prayer and full of faith.

Mr. Rexford A. Boda is President Emeritus at Nyack College, Nyack, New York.

	Student
CHAPTER	**Praying**
14	*by Leslie K. Morgan*

I T HAS BEEN SAID THAT "when God has a plan that requires dedication for 'the long haul,' He often taps on a teenager's shoulder, and asks, 'How about you?' "

Historically, the Lord has always had teenagers whose lives were marked for holiness. These committed youth have blazed new trails for godliness. They have been noted for their power resource in prayer and deep consecration to the Holy Spirit.

The Scriptures record several illustrations of teens whose dedicated lives ushered in divine work and authority. In Daniel 1:8 we read, "But Daniel resolved not to defile himself with the royal food and wine, and he asked the chief official for permission not to defile himself this way."

At approximately age 15, Daniel was removed from his family, culture, a familiar language, friends and all he had ever known, and forced into slavery by a godless nation that had invaded Israel. Yet, Daniel resolved to remain godly. The result of this resolution shook the Babylonian kingdom, impacting at least three successive monarchies.

Esther and Joseph

Esther 4:16 affirms the heart of another young person whose life was set aside exclusively for the Lord: "Go, gather together all the Jews who are in Susa, and fast for me. Do not eat or drink for three days, night or day. I and my maids will fast as you do. When this is done, I will go to the king, even though it is against the law. And if I perish, I perish." The consequence of Esther's godly focus resulted in the saving of the entire Jewish nation.

A third example of a godly younger person was Joseph. At age 17 his brothers sold him into slavery. He was removed from his father's care, his culture, native language and country. Yet, as Daniel, Joseph stayed true to the Lord. Neither temptation of the fiercest caliber from Mrs. Potiphar, rejection and further jail sentencing, nor the granting of the loftiest position in Egypt second only to Pharaoh, could remove Joseph's personal commitment to honor God.

The outcome is recorded for the generations that followed: "You intended to harm me, but God intended it for good to accomplish what is now being done, the saving of many lives" (Genesis 50:20). What began in the life of a person who would today be a junior in high school concluded in the preservation for an entire nation.

Mary

Another example of God using a teenager is found in the New Testament. Galatians 4:4 reminds us that ". . . when the time had fully come, God sent his Son, born of a woman. . . ." The woman selected by God to bring the Savior into the world was Mary (approximately 15–17 years old). Her pure servanthood to God occasioned her being chosen as the one who would bring God's global plan of salvation to mankind. Of all the methods God could have chosen to deliver the package of grace to the world, His choice was a teenage girl.

There are other scriptural examples of teenagers whose walks with the Lord were notable. David was 17 when he was assigned the sacred task of serving the King of Israel.

Paul met a young man with a heart for God. The result was that Timothy was personally discipled by the one who wrote half of the New Testament.

Samuel and Ruth were both young when the Lord began works in their lives that impacted future generations.

While on earth the Lord Jesus had one person who could be called his "best friend." The apostle John was the youngest of the disciples. He was given the care of Mary, the mother of Jesus, he played a significant role in the founding of the church after Pentecost, and he later wrote five books of the New Testament.

From these and other examples, we find that God isn't afraid to use teens in notable measure. While not all adolescent people are worthy of such calls, it is apparent that God isn't embarrassed to give some teens a high profile role within the church.

Albert B. Simpson

Historically, The Christian and Missionary Alliance has seen God call students from within its ranks into powerful ministries. As these young men and women stayed pure in their walks with Christ, they made many spiritual inroads into Satan's territory.

Our founder, A.B. Simpson, is an example. As a young man he was devoted to times of deep prayer and recorded how the Lord confirmed His Spirit within him. Within a few short years after adolescence, Simpson was a noted preacher of the gospel in Canada. From there he moved to Louisville, Kentucky, where again he had a powerful ministry which led to the salvation of many people. The church saw exceptional growth, numerically and spiritually. Later Simpson moved to New York City, where under the impulse of the Holy Spirit he launched a powerful ministry that is still on the cutting edge of world-wide missions. This global impact has its roots in the early devotion of a young man who sought the Lord in fullness and power and prayer.

Richard Harvey

Another notable teen who grew up in The Christian and Missionary Alliance was Richard Harvey. The son of an Alliance pastor, Harvey received the admonition of the Lord from his parents at an early age. Though he resisted the call of the Lord at first, as a young man in his late teen years Richard submitted to the Holy Spirit. He tells of those times he spent in prayer seeking the fullness of the Holy Spirit and asking God to give him power for ministry. In his autobiography, *70 Years of Miracles,* Harvey documents how the Lord answered those prayers, giving him outstanding miraculous events confirming that he was indeed serving the living and powerful Almighty God.

In his book, Harvey tells "The Flask Story." A young man dared to challenge his professor who lectured annually on the subject, "Why God Doesn't Answer Prayer." During the lectures, Harvey said, this college sophomore courageously responded to the professor's invitation to pray aloud that a glass flask held at shoulder height would not break when dropped on the concrete floor. After a brief prayer by the young man, the professor released the flask. Though the professor held the flask directly out in front of him, it fell on his shoe, rolling onto the floor, without damage. The professor, who had given the series of blasphemous lectures for several years before that event, never did so again.

Youth for Christ

Harvey also was one of the founders of Youth for Christ. While living in St. Louis, he was deeply impressed by the Lord to begin a youth-oriented outreach. He and the founding committee began to ask the Lord for ways to influence young people. The Lord sent Billy Graham to the group and Youth for Christ was instantly a hit among young people all across America. Today, Youth for Christ remains a flourishing para-church ministry, reaching thousands of young men and women.

Billy Graham

At age 15, Billy Graham came to know Christ as his Savior while living in Charlotte, North Carolina. He soon felt the call of the Lord into evangelism. After completing high school, he attended the Florida Bible Institute near Tampa. The pastor of the Alliance church in Tampa was John Mender. He had been asking the Lord for a man to lead the young people in his church. Soon after, Billy Graham was introduced to Pastor Mender and became the youth director for the church. It has been historically documented that Billy Graham has made the single most significant impact for Christ since the Apostle Paul. It is also significant to realize that this man, as a young college student, began his ministry in an Alliance church.

A.W. Tozer

A.W. Tozer has been recognized around the world as a 20th century prophet of God. His writings span denominational lines, and his preaching has stirred many to holiness. As a teen, he sought to fill the void in his spirit by seeking God. His quest in those days was fulfilled when, as a young man, he met the Lord in a powerful way. Later, as an adult, he impacted the world with his writings and preaching.

When Tozer pastored the Southside Alliance Church in Chicago, a young teenage girl named Esther attended the fellowship. Her heart for the Lord was impressive to many and she had the single desire of walking in holiness with Christ. Her passion was prayer and purity. Believing the Lord was calling her into missions, she attended Nyack College and began preparing for the Lord's service. She later married Louis King. Together the Kings served the Lord in India and were privileged to see many come to Christ. While Alliance history records substantial spiritual and numerical growth under the presidency of Dr. King, it is interesting to see the hand of God in the background of the King family. As teenagers, God called both Dr. and Mrs. King into full-time ministry. Their impact has been seen throughout the world.

The Sutera Twins

In the early '70s, Western Canada experienced a

tremendous revival of the Holy Spirit. Repentance was widespread, and salvation of the unconverted came to an all-time high. Both pastors and laity were quickened spiritually, acknowledging their need for the fullness of the Holy Spirit. Power flowed back into the churches as in the days of Jonathan Edwards and Charles Finney.

At the hub of this revival were twin brothers, Lou and Ralph Sutera. While their ministries as adult men have seen the obvious blessing of God, it is significant to note that they began preaching as teenagers. They were 16 years old when they first began their ministry, and still today they are holding revivals anointed by the Holy Spirit. Once again, history demonstrates that when God wants to do something for the long-haul, he often taps on the shoulder of a teenager and asks, "How about you?"

A Chain of Prayer

The same call to prayer and holiness heard by young people in the scriptures and in the early days of The Christian and Missionary Alliance is still being heard today. This same God who called the Daniels, Esthers, Josephs and Marys of Bible times is pleased to find there are those now whose ears are as tuned to hear His voice. There are many examples of this throughout our society.

One such sample came from a classroom in one of our colleges. The professor encouraged the students to pray bold prayers with specific requests that could be documented. The class began to record answers to prayer on six-inch strips of paper and linked them together, forming a chain. Within the semester, the class of 20 students saw over 600 specific answers to prayer. The next term the professor spoke in a chapel service, presenting the "prayer chain" as an object lesson in faith. The chain extended half again the length of a regulation basketball court! Indeed, these 20 students who believed God for healings, salvation, protection, finances, restored marriages, miracles and power saw God respond in an exceptional fashion.

An Amazing Answer to Prayer

Another example of students responding to the call of God to prayer is noted from the Campus Community Church at Toccoa Falls College. A couple who attended that church discovered in the seventh month of the wife's pregnancy that she was going to have twins. The next day she went into labor, and the baby boys were born two months premature with severe respiratory difficulties. The babies were rushed to a hospital in Atlanta and were given a limited chance of survival.

Three days later the physician attending the babies called the couple in Toccoa, urging them to come to the hospital. The message was that she doubted the boys would be alive upon the parent's arrival an hour and a half later. The husband called the pastor, asking for the elders to pray for a miracle because the children were requiring pure oxygen for survival. Immediately the elders and pastor assembled themselves together for prayer. Having prayed for approximately an hour, a sense of rest came over the meeting. It was as if the student elders and pastor had completed their assignment.

Arriving at Eagleston Hospital in Atlanta, the parents were greeted by the doctor who stood awestruck at what had just occurred before her very eyes. She told the couple that in all of her years of practice she had never seen one baby respond the way she had just witnessed *both* children respond.

The babies she said, had received "a surge of power."

Their respiratory systems began functioning in full force. The couple asked when this had occurred. The doctor said at approximately 1:15 that afternoon. The prayer meeting had concluded at 1:00! Though at death's door for the first week of life with little chance of survival anticipated, both boys today are healthy pre-schoolers, and their parents are pastoring in Alabama.

Another Answer

The student movement of prayer continues to grow and power is being seen in unprecedented ways. In November of 1992, a student at Toccoa Falls College was discovered to have a brain tumor. The campus pastor, college president and dean led the student body in prayer, asking God to work supernaturally on behalf of the student. In their classes and private devotions, the students continued to pray throughout the week.

On the day surgery was scheduled, the physicians wanted to have final X-rays for accuracy in the operation. To their amazement, they could find no tumor at all, though they had previous X-rays to prove there had been a mass.

The scheduled surgery was completely unnecessary, and the young man returned home for a joyous Christmas season with his family. The students give credit to the Lord for intervening in behalf of their fellow student and believe God answered in a specific way in power!

A Remarkable Turnaround

The prayer movement among students in The Christian and Missionary Alliance has not been confined to just a particular region but is being seen nationally. One such example is noted from what occurred at Delta Lake Camp in Rome, New York, in 1990.

At the family camp that year, a 15-year-old who had not wanted to be there was obstinate and antagonistic about attending the meetings. He even vowed to his mother that he was going to look into becoming a Satanist upon his arrival back home.

Several students linked spiritual arms together throughout the week, asking the Lord to soften the boy's hard heart. The Lord began to do so in a supernatural fashion. Toward the end of the week, the speaker gave a challenging word from Scripture about salvation. The young man was obviously stirred by the conviction of the Holy Spirit and at the end of the message, he was the first one at the altar, where he knelt and received Jesus Christ as his Lord. It was a direct answer to the prayers of the other teens who faithfully pounded heaven's door, pleading for this young man to come to Christ.

But there was more! The next night the speaker spoke on serving God in full-time ministry. At the invitation the same young man was so moved by the grace of God for saving him that he responded to the wooing of the Holy Spirit and consecrated his life to Christ.

How did this once rebellious, hard-headed, hard-hearted young man who vowed to consider Satanism come to do a 180-degree turnabout? We believe it was a specific response by God as fellow students interceded on his behalf and refused to quit until they saw the demonstration of the Holy Spirit's power in their midst. That is exactly what they received!

"See You at the Pole"

Christian and Missionary Alliance students are likewise credited for being part of the *See You at the Pole* prayer movement on September 16, 1992. Junior and senior high schools all across America saw students gather at the flagpoles of their campuses for prayer. It is estimated that three million students were praying on that day for spiritual renewal, the salvation of their friends and for a spiritual awakening on their campuses.

The Life '92 conference held at Fort Collins, Colorado in August had a special concert of prayer for the *See You at the Pole* effort. The tremendous success of having three million students participating throughout the United States can be credited in part to the prayer support of students at Life '92.

The haystack group at Toccoa Falls College has also challenged people within the ranks of the Alliance. As many as 50 students have practiced fasting and praying during the Wednesday noon meal, setting aside that hour to intercede for the needs of missionaries and pastors throughout the world. Much gratitude has been expressed globally for this prayer support. Similar groups have been started on other Alliance campuses, where much spiritual work is being accomplished for the glory of God.

God Calls Yet

God is neither reluctant nor afraid to call students

to pray and to minister. He will enable them with power from the Holy Spirit. Our roots within the Alliance include people who have responded to this sacred call. They have impacted thousands for Christ's sake because they first sought God in prayer.

This present generation faces unprecedented levels of spiritual darkness and evil. Many of the students of The Christian and Missionary Alliance are not ashamed to follow in the pattern of our Alliance "fore-parents." They are responding to the truth that "when God has a plan that requires dedication for 'the long haul,' He often taps on a teenager's shoulder and asks, 'How about you?' "

Rev. Leslie K. Morgan is the Senior Pastor at the Campus Community Church, Toccoa Falls, Georgia.

CHAPTER	Women
15	at Prayer

Women at Prayer

by Charlotte Stemple

IT WAS OVER 100 DEGREES and the fan was barely turning overhead. As I faced my tutor across the desk I could not hear the difference in what he was saying from what I was striving to repeat, apparently unsuccessfully. Would I *ever* learn this tonal language? Would all my preparation for missions be in vain, stalled by this slow process which turned an otherwise competent adult into a social child? And was it worth it? Could I measure the progress at all after these many weeks? Oh, yes, I followed the message last Sunday and even found the pages in the hymnal as they were announced. And bargaining in the market was beginning to be fun. Maybe, just maybe, there *was* hope!

ANITA: In 1976 I read an *Alliance Witness* article by a missionary to Vietnam. She and her husband were forced to leave because of the war. They elected to serve in the Philippines. The article stressed the difficulty and need for prayer in learning a new language. My heart was touched and I decided to faithfully pray for those undertaking this challenging task. I gradually added others until today I pray through the whole prayer directory. God has been so faithful to answer many, many of my requests for His servants. How blessed I am.

CHAR AGAIN: The small boy ran across the hospital yard to our house next door. He was frantic. His mother had just died in childbirth and his father was far away serving in the military; now the hospital was demanding that he take the body. How and where could he take his dear mother? Since my husband was away, I made an instant decision; yes, I would help this child. Driving my van to the small shed called the morgue, arranging with the carpenter for a simple red wooden casket, loading the casketed body in the back and the small boy beside me, we started out to the distant village where we would put the boy and his mother in the charge of the local pastor. The road was dangerous; much of it had been blown away by road mines. When we came to a wide creek, I saw the bridge was gone and had been replaced by some metal planks and a few logs wired together. I would have to negotiate this treacherous crossing with the little boy going ahead on foot and directing my car to the right or left to keep it exactly on the crossing paths, just wide enough for the wheels of my van. Was I able for this? Weeks later I was incredibly touched when the soldier-father came home on leave, heard the story from his pastor and humbly stood at my door with a bag of fresh duck eggs to say "thank you" for my help in that difficult moment of their sorrow.

JEAN: My daily life is full of pressing responsibilities, making a lengthy prayer time for our missionaries very difficult. However, I find that throughout the hours of my day there are many opportunities to bring our missionaries and their ministry to the Lord in prayer. I like to call this type of praying, "Situation Praying." As I find myself in various situations, I can pray right then for a missionary going through the same thing. For example, often as I travel I am reminded of a missionary and the dangerous traveling and traffic situations he or she is in. In times of sickness, loneliness or weariness in ministry, I remember a missionary who may be experiencing the same thing. When I have inadequate means or lack proper tools to do a job, I pray for the missionary who is having to "make do." Visiting various mission fields and seeing the missionaries in the midst of their ministries has helped me to visualize a missionary and engage in "situational praying." This is not a substitute for personal study and prayer time, but it does help me avoid simply praying, "Bless the missionaries."

CHAR AGAIN: I lay in bed in our Danang home in tears. My senior missionary had just brought me home from the local hospital after again experiencing the miscarriage of a greatly-desired child. My helpless husband tried to console me as I cried for my mother, 12,000 miles away. How many times would this grief of child loss shatter us? Would God *ever* grant the desire of our hearts for children? "Not my will, but Thine" is not an easy prayer, but only in resignation is release, as so many before us already knew.

MIRIAM: Much of my growth in my prayer life has come through times of physical testing. Lying alone on a hospital bed I have been lifted into the heavenlies through meditation on who God is until my heart is at peace in His love and goodness.

GRACE: Sometimes God uses circumstances in our lives to lay on our hearts a burden for others. Since having cancer, the Lord has increasingly led me to pray especially for those who have health needs. This intercession has included many missionaries and Christian workers. All have not been healed, but I am sure God has granted comfort, peace and guidance in answer to prayer.

CHAR AGAIN: As the missionaries met in conference, God answered far beyond our expectations.

Revival occurred as the Holy Spirit fell on dry and seeking hearts; confessions, reconciliations and restitutions took place, and renewed power for ministry was outpoured. From there it spread to the Vietnamese Bible School and out into the churches. I will never forget being part of a journey deeper and deeper into God's blessing and I know He prepared *us* as well as the Vietnamese church by His gracious signs and presence for the wrath of war soon to be outpoured on that country.

LESLIE: The past 14 months have truly been a journey into prayer for me. God began leading me into a more committed prayer life; praying for missionaries, missions and lost men and women began to be an explosive time when God's presence became so overwhelming that it was ever more noticeable than my physical surroundings. He showed me how important it was to pray through a burden that was given directly by the Holy Spirit, for when that burden was lifted I could know for sure that someone had gained victory, had been set free from Satan's bondage or had come to know the Lord. I tell you that prevailing intercession has been the most explosive force I have ever experienced. It has brought me ever closer to God. It has conformed my desires to be more like the Lord. As a result, God has dealt with areas of my life that I had never seemed able to gain victory in. A little over a year after this whole process began, God took me a step further into His truth. After three days of prayer, God brought me to surrender areas of my heart that I have never been willing to give to Him before. He brought to my mind specific sins. The most difficult to deal with was pride. After four days of nothing but prayer, I was experiencing God's protection, power, cleansing and guidance in a mighty way. I can only pray that others will not be willing to settle for an empty, powerless prayer life, but rather will take a step of faith into the realm of the heavenly that we do not have to wait to get to heaven to see.

CHAR AGAIN: This time when the fighting erupted it was very close. Flares lit the night sky with surreal brightness as explosions shook the house and tracer bullets visibly punctuated the rat-a-tat of nearby machine guns. We had been told by the embassy to go to the fortified house down the street if ground fighting broke out. Were we safer crouching in our bedroom bunker or making a dash down the strangely empty street? My husband chose: he picked up our infant son and the always-packed emergency suitcase and reached for my hand as we opened the door—breathing a fast prayer as we went. In all our war-ravaged days in Vietnam, that was the *only* time that a bullet went through our living room and lodged in our wall.

WINNIE: I became a praying woman after accepting the Lord in the '50s. That was when the Lord was opening up New Guinea (now called Irian Jaya), and it was thrilling to follow God's marvelous working there. I have always had a desire to visit that field and have never had the opportunity, but a missionary friend told me I had claimed a lot of that island on my knees. I never forgot that. One night more recently I awoke with a real prayer burden for a certain missionary in Burkina Faso. I wrote to her, telling of this experience; she wrote back that there was nothing she could remember on that date but then she noted something very important: no one would ever know what was *averted* through those prayers.

CHAR AGAIN: Thursday was one of my favorite days. Because it was a day off from school I spent the morning teaching children. They were so eager to listen and learn, and they were always waiting when my bicycle arrived at their makeshift chapel door. As refugees proliferated in our little town, so the children's classes bloomed until I was teaching those "old, familiar stories" to nearly a thousand children each week. To most of them it was all new and fresh and so easy to apply in their own eastern culture. And memorize! The children thrilled my heart (and strained my supply of recycled greeting

214

card prizes) with their eagerness to show how many verses they had learned. From the schoolrooms to the prisons we would go on Thursday afternoons; at one point visiting three prisons each week, but saving the "big house" for Thursdays when our whole ministry team could go. God set many men and women free within those walls on Thursdays. What a busy, yet exhilarating day. Why did I always feel so empowered for ministry from morning till night? Could it be because the time zone differences made our Thursdays still Wednesdays "back home" where the Prayer Directory and the prayer meetings were often turned to the Vietnam requests?

BEV: Some people are called to be pastors, some missionaries, some Sunday school teachers. Some are called to other fields of service. A few years ago the Lord called me to use the Prayer Directory of The Christian and Missionary Alliance. When I first started praying for the missionaries, I had a hard time praying for someone I had never met or seen. When we had the picture box of cards, I began to put the cards with the Directory and could actually put names with faces; then their families and their work came alive for me. When I am not working I am up very early in the morning using my Prayer Directory. I like to commit the pastors and people of the districts to the Lord and ask His presence, blessing and direction for them as they awaken. Do the missionaries have the assurance that we are holding them up in prayer? I heard one say, "If I didn't believe God's people were praying for me, I wouldn't *dare* go back to the field." I thank the Lord for allowing me to be involved in His work through prayer.

CHAR AGAIN: Our firstborn was now six. Before he was born we promised him to the Lord; as he grew we daily committed him to God. Now the day of our commitment was to be tested—the day to send him off to boarding school in far-away Penang. He was so excited he couldn't wait. At long last he could go with all the other kids to the "promised land" called Dalat School. And so he went. Only God knows how our hearts yielded at that moment; we can only testify that His grace was sufficient. That surrender was not in defeat; it was in victory as we took our own hands off our son (and later his brother) and watched God use other godly people to help us mold and shape his life for Jesus. What an awesome privilege to have many people praying for our little family of four; how wonderful that these long-desired boys have an extended family of aunts and uncles whom they visit all over the world—plus many they have not yet met—who have invested in their lives. We are truly blessed.

NANCY: One day I received a letter from a dear

missionary friend. I could almost hear her sobbing as she wrote of a 23-year-old MK home in the United States by herself feeling God had let her down and did not love her. My friend wrote, ". . . you have a mother's heart. I want you to minister to her." It would have been easy had this girl known me or lived nearby. She didn't; she lived over 1,000 miles away. Satan would have me put the letter aside and do nothing, but I knew God wanted me to respond. As I went to prayer, Satan kept taunting me with excuses why she wouldn't want to talk with me and I shouldn't phone her. It was a miracle how I got her number at college, but then as I dialed I hoped she wouldn't be in. When she answered the phone she was very quiet, but I persisted in telling her why I was calling and how I cared for her and would be praying. In a step of faith I also told her to call me "collect" any time of the day or night. From then on I would talk to her or write her or send her a funny clipping or an encouraging note a few times each week. Finally after a few months I received a note from her. She could not believe someone cared for her and took time for her. Her parents came home on furlough about six months later and the burden was lifted from my heart. I praise God for the privilege of bringing that lonely girl to the throne of grace and sharing so deeply in her life.

CHAR AGAIN: When I came home on furlough, I loved the interaction with the people in Alliance churches. We took every opportunity to speak and share what God was doing in our lives and on our field. How incredible to meet many who told us they had "prayed for us every single day we were gone." Near the end of the year, the schedule got hectic; there were days when we separated to minister in two different places. Getting the children ready for yet another service (or yet another nursery) and finding new material to encourage people who had heard us speak in other settings already was really "too much." I well remember the Sunday when the oldest said, "Do I have to be a visitor again?" Yet, whenever we arrived at the appointed place, God never failed to bless *us*, in spite of our weariness.

LYNNE: I don't think I have achieved "prayer warrior" status yet. I believe I am a "prayer warrior in progress." I am pleased to report that my growth in prayer *began* when I joined the Alliance church three years ago. So, the first step in becoming prayer conscious is to become part of a praying body of believers. They offered me two things in particular: (1) opportunity to pray and hear prayer and (2) individual role models. My personal prayer life has grown as I have become less self-minded and more people-minded. I find this to be especially true when it comes to praying for missionaries. When I get to know them personally through missions conferences, they become real people in real places working with real people with real needs. When I read their names in *Alliance Life* magazine (a real informing *life* line for me), I can relate to their circumstances and remember them in prayer again. Many Scriptures have also taught me to pray; Romans 8:26–27 has been especially comforting when I have felt that I do not know how to pray for a particular circumstance. Instead of *not* praying, I just sit quietly and think about the person and lift his or her name to the Lord who knows what to do with that concern! The most important thing in becoming a "prayer warrior" is the development of a real, growing, personal relationship with God the Father—knowing Him as *Abba*; knowing that He cares for me, loves me and is always there for me and listens to my prayer. Praying is no longer a task when I have that relationship. It is a conversation with a loved One who has the power to change lives and is just waiting for me to ask!

CHAR AGAIN: As furlough progressed we realized we had to do a chore none of us particularly relished—get a family picture taken and prayer cards made. Scheduling a suitable appointment time, agreeing on a pose we all liked, deciding how many to have printed and finding funds to pay for them were just the first of the problems. What size should the card be? What address should we use? How could ours be practical and different so it wouldn't be tossed out, but *used*? We settled on a five-year folding wallet calendar and encouraged people to circle each day they prayed for us, saying we would inspect them when we got back!

LUCY: When I started going to women's meetings God gave me a burden for our missionaries, so I started supporting and praying for them. It has been a real joy. A verse I read on a prayer card says it all to me: "I urge you, brothers, by our Lord Jesus Christ and by the love of the Spirit, to join me in my struggle by praying to God for me" (Romans 15:30).

CHAR AGAIN: It was almost Christmas and the most evangelistic of seasons in Vietnam. Many programs were planned which would include our extensive support, travel and involvement. Every church was excited about the outreach to non-Christians which would take place at this truly Christian holiday time. Among the pile of Christmas cards which came in the mail, we received a letter from the National Office; due to a budgetary shortfall, we would have to go on the dreaded "pro rata." This not only meant that missionary allowances would be cut by a uniform percentage all over the world, but also *our projects* would be cut by that same percentage. What hard choices would this involve, and what lost opportunities? Almost the very next mail brought the unbelievable news that Alliance people had responded with a generous outpouring that would restore the proposed cuts and enable us to end the year with the projects funded. What great rejoicing!

DORIS: People's examples have had a big influence on me regarding prayer. I could not believe my ears (and eyes, because I peeked) when I heard a *layman* freely praying at the Alliance church when I first attended in 1976. I was used to only hearing prayers *read* by the pastor of the formal church I had attended. Before I would join up seriously with this new church, I decided to check out a Wednesday night prayer meeting. I thought I had died and gone to heaven when I saw a prominent leader *down on his knees* by his chair crying out to God for financial needs. His God was real and alive; mine was the distant God of the Old Testament. I had a great desire to be like this praying man. Later I could not understand how two women could faithfully pray by using the Prayer Directory; to me it was like a telephone book, so dry, but I longed to intercede like they did. By example, these people duplicated themselves and their prayer passions in me without ever knowing it; praying daily, and respectfully, and believingly, and in an orderly way—keeping on, keeping on. *People praying* have influenced me.

CHAR AGAIN: We go through seasons of life where needs and opportunities are different, but we are always in need of prayer. When does the "prayer-recipient" become the "prayer-giver" and how do we measure our prayers' effects and those of others? We will never fully understand the mystery of prayer—how the voice of man can effect change through God's dealings with ourselves and others—but we believe it is the most powerful weapon or tool at our disposal. We are profoundly grateful for those who have prayed for us, and we want to do our part in prayer for others. God has honored prayers. The little boy who went off to Dalat School is back in his beloved Asia as a member of IFAP (International Fellowship of Alliance Professionals). (It was no easier saying goodbye to him last month than it was 20 years ago.) His "little brother" now has a lovely wife and people call him "Pastor," and we thank God for hearing prayer and for working out His purpose. I have, in a sense, come full circle in my prayer life; may I be found faithful by following the best advice I have ever had about prayer: *Do it, do it, do it!*

A former missionary to Vietnam, Mrs. Charlotte Stemple is a retreat and conference speaker from Rome, New York. Her husband, Woody, is the district superintendent of the Northeastern District.

Men at Prayer

by R. Stanley Tam

ABOUT 20 YEARS AGO AN Inter-
Varsity representative, visiting in my
office, asked a strange question.

"Mr. Tam, do you have any friends?"

"I have a lot of friends," I answered.

"Do you have one true friend?"

"What do you mean?"

"Well, suppose you fell into sin or you went into
bankruptcy or an accident left you a hopeless cripple. Do you have a friend who would stick with you
through thick and thin?"

"No-o-o," I reflected slowly. "I guess I don't have
a friend like that."

"Mr. Tam, there is a movement going across our
country in which men like you have a prayer
partner. And ladies, too, have a prayer partner. You
would meet at least once a week and pray together
for each other."

Then he proceeded to explain the philosophy behind the idea.

"Every Christian has a weak side. *You* have a weak

side. That is where Satan always attacks. But if you have a prayer partner, your weakness will probably be his strength and his weakness will probably be your strength. The Bible speaks about one chasing a thousand and two putting 10,000 to flight. When you have a prayer partner you become 10 times stronger!"

It sounded logical.

"If you read the Word of God," my friend continued, "you will find prayer partners all the way through the Scriptures. Moses had Aaron, David had Jonathan, Paul had Silas. Christ did not send out His disciples one by one. Had He done so, all of them might have returned defeated. He sent them out two by two and they returned victorious saying, 'Even the demons submit to us in your name.' The Scriptures also say, 'Again, I tell you that if two of you on earth agree about anything you ask for, it will be done for you by my Father in heaven'" (Matthew 18:19).

I Phoned a Friend

My InterVarsity friend so challenged me that I telephoned a business friend.

"Art," I said, "I must have lunch with you today. I have something to talk to you about." And over lunch I explained the whole proposal to Art and asked him if he would be willing to be my prayer partner.

"Tam," he replied, "I believe this is of God. I will make a covenant with you for one year." It is a covenant which we have renewed year after year.

We meet on Thursdays over at the city park in his automobile or mine, where no telephone can interrupt our prayer time. I pray for Art. Art prays for me. I pray for his business. He prays for mine. I pray for his family. He prays for mine.

But there in the city park God put it upon our hearts to ask Him for a ministry.

And in the Lord's leading we began a Bible class at the plant I manage. It was a neutral place where the lost were not reluctant to come and study the Word of God. And over the years we have seen more than 100 people come to know Christ as we have studied the Word with them and talked to them about Jesus Christ.

That was one ministry which God led us to begin as Art and I prayed together. The second was to put tract racks in all the self-service laundries in the area. We now have racks in 19 different locations. Women who come to wash their clothes have at least 10 minutes in which to read. More than 900,000 gospel tracts have been taken and people have been saved.

One Saturday afternoon as I returned home from work my wife met me at the door.

"A man has been calling you all day," she said. "He seems to be very concerned about something. I told him to call back at a quarter to five." Sure enough, at a quarter to five the telephone rang.

"Mr. Tam," the voice on the other end of the wire pleaded, "I just must talk to you tonight!"

"All right," I replied. "I will be free at 9:30. Come to my home." At exactly 9:30 he was at the door. He turned out to be the brother of the chief of police in our city.

"Mr. Tam, since last October I've had marital trouble. This means that I've had to do my own laundry. I've been going to the laundromat on North Cole Street and I've been reading the tracts from your rack there.

"I've been driving around all day today. Each time I've called your home it's been from a different place. Mr. Tam, the only thing I want is to be born again. I want to know Jesus Christ as my Savior. I've come to the end of my strength. Either I give my life to Christ today or I will commit suicide."

I had the privilege of leading that man to Christ in my home that night. When I gave him his coat as he prepared to leave, I felt his pocket. Sure enough, there was a revolver in the pocket. How glad I was that he had chosen to give his life to Christ rather than to take his life.

Prayer Encounter

As my friend Art and I continued our prayer encounters in the city park, the Lord impressed upon us that maybe there was the possibility of starting a Christian radio station in our city. We inquired and learned that a channel was open in our area. For several years now our Christian radio station has been on the air with the gospel 24 hours a day, seven days a week.

One Thursday as I met my prayer partner I found him brokenhearted.

"Stanley," he began, "my son has fallen in love with a girl of another faith. Now he's engaged. I told him he could do anything but marry an unsaved girl. I told him I would not continue to finance his law school education, but the girl's father owns the telephone company and is willing to put my son through college."

What do you do in a situation like that? You cannot reason with someone in love. And the family he was marrying into was well-to-do.

"Art," I said, "we can bind Satan. We can resist the devil. And we can stand on the promise that 'if two of you on earth agree about any thing you ask for, it will be done for you by my Father in heaven.' "

So we did just that. Week after week. And just before the wedding, the engagement was broken off. Just like that. Today Art's son has completed law school and is married to a born-again Christian girl.

Getting results from prayer, said George Mueller—perhaps the greatest man of faith that ever lived—is quoting God's promises from the Bible back to Him and saying, "You said it. I believe it, and I am not giving up until you answer."

But quoting (His promises) back to God may not always be the solution in getting your prayers answered. God is basically interested in doing business with clean vessels. Difficulties may come into our lives just to get us to clean up our lives. "Dear friends, if our hearts do not condemn us, we have confidence before God" (1 John 3:21). But, let's turn that Scripture around. If we get down on our knees and our hearts condemn us, then we have no confidence that He will answer our prayers. Action must be taken in this area before we see answers to our prayers.

Preventative Maintenance

Then there is another consideration. Have you ever thought that God has methods of "preventive maintenance" in our Christian lives? By using these methods we can eliminate a great host of our problems, disappointments and reverses. Here are a couple of ways to do it.

"In [Jesus Christ] are hidden all the treasures of wisdom and knowledge" (Colossians 2:3). Make it a habit every morning—yes, *every* morning—to ask God for divine wisdom and knowledge to make divine decisions. Then ask God to do the same for every family member and for those whom you work with. You will immediately see a great reduction in your problems.

Secondly, think it over—you have only one enemy. Since he has lost you out of his family, he has only one goal for you—to cripple you and make you useless for Christ. Make it a habit of every morning—yes, *every* morning—to bind the devil by the Word of God, the blood of Jesus and by the authority invested in you as a Christian. "Whatever you bind on earth will be bound in heaven" (Matthew 18:18). Then name every member of your family, your home, your car, your vocation, your social life, your investments and the people you work with. You will immediately see many of your problems disappear. You should bind the devil out loud because he is not omniscient. Some believe he cannot hear or understand silent prayer. Do it while you are in the bathroom or driving to work.

Pete Peterson

Perhaps the most difficult object of those Thursday prayer times was a man by the name of Pete Peterson. Pete lived right there in Lima, Ohio. His wife went to the same church I did. She had married Pete while she was backslidden, and when she returned to the Lord she had an unsaved husband on her hands. For 15 years she had prayed for him and urged him to go to church. For 15 years Pete had resisted. Pete Peterson was not interested in spiritual things. He was an alcoholic and a chain smoker.

For one whole year we prayed for Pete Peterson. Just about then Pete and his wife sold everything and moved to California. It certainly did not look as if our if-any-two-of-you-shall-agree verse was working.

But then we decided that God could save Pete Peterson in California as easily as in Ohio, and we continued to pray.

About three months later I received an invitation to go to California to speak at a men's retreat. My wife was immediately excited.

"Stanley," she said, "God is sending you to California to lead Pete to Christ!" My prayer partner agreed.

"But California is a big state," I objected. "I don't know where the Petersons live and I don't even know exactly where the retreat is being held."

"I'm going to find out," my wife promised. And one evening as I returned from work she had a map of California spread out on the kitchen table.

"I found both places," my wife announced triumphantly. "They are seven miles apart!"

So she wrote to Mrs. Peterson, and as soon as I got out to California on Friday, I telephoned her.

"This is so exciting!" Mrs. Peterson exclaimed. "Tomorrow morning is the first half-day we've had off since we went into this business. Would you come over as early as you possibly can? I'll make sure Pete is here."

I took another layman with me, Steve Lazarian, from Pasadena. We drove over to the little town where the Peterson's lived.

As we talked with Pete about Jesus Christ we could sense the presence of God in that living room. For two hours we talked.

"Pete," I said finally, "you have run as far from God as you possibly can. I think this morning is the time you should give your heart to Jesus Christ."

Pete look resigned. "You're right, Mr. Tam. I'm licked. I can't run any farther."

That morning as we knelt together in the Peterson living room, Pete gave his heart to Christ. That evening we picked him up and took him to the men's retreat where he gave his first public testimony that he was now a child of God.

A few weeks after I had returned home Mrs. Peterson called us.

"Stanley," she announced soberly, "Pete is dead. He was down at the gas station the other morning and there was a holdup. Someone fired a revolver and the bullet went through Pete's head. He died almost instantly.

"But," she continued with a note of triumph, "although I've lost my husband, I am rejoicing because Pete gave a testimony that he was born again, and I shall see him when I get to heaven."

A few days later she wrote me a letter. "We buried Pete in San Diego, where my brother lives. During the funeral God saved my brother. I am rejoicing because my husband and my brother were won to Christ."

Jesus said, "If *two of you* on earth agree about anything you ask, it will be done for you by my Father in heaven."

If God has spoken to you about having a prayer partner, why not take immediate steps to get one?

Dr. Stanley Tam is President of U.S. Plastics, Lima, Ohio.

	Prayer for
CHAPTER	**Families**
17	
	by H. Robert and Marjorie Cowles

I T IS NOT NEWS THAT THE Christian family finds itself under severe Satanic attack. The entertainment industry, the electronic and print media, even government have joined forces to do it in. And they are succeeding.

Satan's war against the Christian family is understandable. The nuclear family is God's basic societal unit. God created the first such family in the Garden of Eden when He made Eve from Adam's rib. Within the genetic structures of that first couple He planned all the billions of families that have followed. More significantly, God decreed the nuclear family as the conveyer of spiritual and social values from generation to generation. To Israel God directed Moses to say:

Hear, O Israel: The LORD our God, the LORD is one. Love the LORD your God with all your heart and with all your soul and with all your strength. These commandments that I give you today are to be upon your hearts. Impress them on your children. Talk about them when you sit at home and when you walk along the road, when you lie down and when you get up. Tie them as symbols on your hands and bind them on your foreheads. Write them on the doorframes of your houses and on your gates. (Deuteronomy 6:4-9)

Paul wrote to Timothy: "I have been reminded of your sincere faith, which first lived in your grandmother Lois and in your mother Eunice and, I am persuaded, now lives in you also" (2 Timothy 1:5). That is how the system is supposed to work.

Little wonder that Satan is doing his utmost to destroy this bastion of spiritual and societal values. If he can destroy the Christian family, he wins the war. It's that black and white.

Parents Need to Pray

Certainly the Christian family needs all the prayer help it can get. But from a practical standpoint we must face the fact that nearly every potential pray-er is involved in a nuclear family of his or her own. While we bear one another's burdens, especially in times of crisis and special need, we cannot in fairness expect others to shoulder, on a regular basis, a major share of *our* prayer responsibility.

We who head a nuclear family unit must therefore take the lead in praying for our own household and those within it. No matter how pressing our work schedule, how demanding our church responsibilities, how weary of body and mind we are, we need to *make* time to pray. Nothing is more urgent; nothing counts for as much.

Praying with our child or children at bedtime may seem like an imposition on our time—the more so if there are several children who go to bed at different hours. But few things we do for our children will make a deeper impression or be remembered with profounder gratitude.

When sickness or accident intrudes, prayer should be our first recourse, not our last. Children are past masters at reading our signals, so we need to be sure we are praying not for show but because we genuinely believe prayer changes things.

That applies also to our private, personal time with God. We do not pray to impress our children, but they will know—and remember—whether these times are regular or haphazard, anticipated or dutiful, refreshing or a burden. Like it or not, we parents are models in nearly everything we do and say.

The *Family* Needs to Pray

Parents need to pray for their household. But the household also needs to participate in prayer. This exercise goes by various names: family altar, family devotions, family prayers. It is the involvement of all members of the nuclear family, from youngest on up, in corporate worship and prayer.

"The family that prays together stays together." There may be exceptions to that catchy slogan, but they are not many. And in a day when even Christian families are not exempt from split-ups, the antidote is timely indeed.

The only winners when a marriage fails are the lawyers. Certainly not the husband or wife, who are haunted by failure, loneliness, anger, disappointment and a whole battery of other negative emotions. Certainly not the children, who are scarred permanently—and often deeply—even though they soon discover their experience is far from unique.

Nothing—repeat, *nothing*—contributes to family cohesion quite as much as family prayer. If keeping the nuclear family intact were its only virtue, family prayer would be worth almost any amount of time and effort. But that is but one of a long list of benefits.

What Our Children Remember

God has blessed the two of us with three daughters and a son. We do *not* set ourselves up as perfect parents. Far from it. We have made our share of blunders. We have fallen well short of the spiritual ideal. (We did excel in one thing: we loved our children dearly—and still do. Never were kids loved more than we loved our kids.) In spite of our deficiencies as parents, however, all four of our children are following the Lord. For that we are profoundly grateful to God.

It's always a bit scary to quiz your adult children about childhood memories, and especially about the spiritual impact their parents may have had (or not had) on their lives. But in preparation for writing this chapter, we did just that.

Do you know what every one of them mentioned first as the most formative influence in her or his life? *Family devotions.* That consistent, daily exercise impacted each of them the most. Not so incidentally, the two of our children with children of their own are following today the same pattern in their homes.

We selected dinner time as most propitious for assembling everyone. Morning schedules ruled out breakfast, and no one was home for lunch. So immediately following dinner, we had devotions, rain or shine, activity or no activity, guests or no guests.

While our children were small, we selected Christian biography—books such as *Young Rebel in Bristol* (George Mueller), *White Queen of the Cannibals* (Mary Slessor), the *Jungle Doctor* series (Paul White)—exciting narratives of model Christians laced with Bible truth. *Young Pilgrim's Progress* was also a favorite.

Was it worthwhile—those daily times of reading and family prayer? Was it worth the effort to consistently carve out time from a family's typical calendar of activities? Yes, yes—a thousand times over!

When Does a Couple Start Family Devotions?

Families should never outgrow family devotions. The husband and wife who made family devotions a normal routine when their children were young will probably continue the practice in later life, finding the exercise both profitable and a pleasure. But when should you *begin* the practice?

1. Ideally, on the evening of your engagement, if you still have that option! Isn't that when you decide to be a "family"? What better way to be assured of God's blessing upon the future years than to together seek His face and His will in the days of serious courtship? Prayer can be a powerful deterrent to the excesses that have blighted, if not blasted, so many courtships.

2. Your honeymoon is an appropriate time to involve God in your lives. You have entered joyously on a joint venture "for better or for worse." After the frenzy of activity surrounding the wedding, the tranquility of your honeymoon setting is the perfect place to thank God for each other, to tell Him that you love Him and to pledge to begin a family altar in your new home.

3. When your first child is conceived. At that

point you begin a new partnership as parents. The experience is unique to you; the responsibility is awesome; more than ever you need God's help. If God can see that "unformed body," if He has written in His book "all the days ordained" for that anticipated baby (Psalm 139:16), surely it is not too soon to begin praying for the new life God is giving you and for the two people most directly responsible for its nurture.

4. Early, very early after the baby arrives. You need to involve that little one in "family" devotions. He or she will not remember, any more than he or she will remember the church services you take him or her to, but the pattern is important to all three of you.

It will be years until your baby begins to understand. And when understanding does begin to come, you'll need to match the material and activity to his or her development. But the point is to begin early the practice of corporate family prayer—not in place of, but in addition to, your personal, daily meeting with God.

Surprising Spiritual Capacity

Rather soon you will discover that your son or daughter has a surprisingly large capacity for God. Cultivate it. Do nothing to quench his or her faith. Be mindful that Jesus declared, "Let the little children come to me, . . . for the kingdom of heaven belongs to such as these" (Matthew 19:14).

As the years move on, your family is certain to face important decisions. Involve God in those decisions through family prayer. Later, your teen will be facing some very profound choices involving higher education, vocation, possibly even marriage. Guide, but do not manipulate or dictate. Make sure he or she clearly understands the options; then let the final decision be his or hers. Meanwhile, pray hard!

Regularly, consistently maintain the pattern of family devotions until the last child is out of the nest. And then? Continue the practice until death stops you. The members of your nuclear family are never beyond the need of your prayers. For 19 centuries Jesus has been interceding for people like us; surely we can and should continue to intercede for the members of our family.

Five Reasons for Family Prayer

There are at least five reasons for corporate family prayer:

1. You are setting a pattern. "Train a child in the way he should go, / and when he is old, he will not turn from it" (Proverbs 22:6).

"But I'm worried that family devotions will become rote," you protest. "They will have no real meaning. They may even turn off my kids."

Did that thought come to you from God or Satan?

"Do not believe every spirit, but test the spirits to see if they are from God" (1 John 4:1). Satan will do whatever he can to discourage you from regular family devotions.

2. You yourself, father or mother, are a model for your children in this matter. Who will be most apt to establish a family altar in his or her home: the one who customarily had such an experience when he or she was growing up, or the one who did not?

3. Your family desperately needs this daily spiritual tryst. From dawn till dark (and beyond), your kids are bombarded with non-Christian values. You and your spouse are not spared from Satanic attack, either. Isaiah's affirmation to God is still wonderfully true: "You will keep in perfect peace / him whose mind is steadfast, / because he trusts in you" (26:3).

4. Your children need to know that God answers prayer. If you approach these daily devotional times seriously and not haphazardly or flippantly, those children God has entrusted to your care are going to see that God means what He says: He answers prayer. And He also inspired the psalmist who said, "The unfolding of your words gives light; / it gives understanding to the simple" (Psalm 119:130).

5. When the time comes for your children to begin a daily quiet time of their own—a very important transition point in their lives—the family altar experience will serve them as a good launch pad

and a good pattern.

Seen, Not Heard

We adults tend not to take kids too seriously, especially other people's. We humor them, tolerate them, feed them, pray for them (if they're sick) and haul them to little league games with our own. But we prefer to talk to adults, and the old adage, "Children should be seen, not heard," has our tacit endorsement.

Maybe we're not too different from Jesus' disciples, who shooed the mothers and children away from Jesus, protesting that He was too busy to be bothered. And if so, we are not very much like Jesus, who invited the children to come to Him, who took them in His arms and blessed them.

Jesus, who knew people's inner thoughts, had great respect for children. He was especially struck by their honest faith. He said we all need to become like little children in order to enter the kingdom of heaven (Matthew 18:3). He loved those Jewish kids then and He loves kids today. He said their angels have continuous access to His Father (18:10). They are among those whom He wants to come to repentance (2 Peter 3:9).

Children Do Grow

But that innocent little toddler becomes the smart

aleck and the braggart and the mischief-maker and finally the know-it-all teen. And if you are the parent of the teen, you wonder with a certain sense of despair if you can survive the next seven years without going completely berserk.

You can find good literature to help you cope—if only you have time to read it. But prayer and patience and prayer and love and prayer and understanding and prayer and commendation and prayer, prayer, prayer are really the only things that can see you through the adolescent years of your children. Try not to lose your sense of humor. But most of all, pray.

The fact is, it is impossible to raise godly children in our modern society without great quantities of prayer. And these years of child-rearing come when fathers and mothers are pressed by careers, by societal demands, by financial decisions, by a legion of extra-curricular responsibilities that militate against quality prayer time.

In what we say next we are not excusing parents from praying. They need to pray. They *must* pray. But how wonderful it would be if a single adult or two could team up with a beleaguered family at wits' end and partner with them in a prayer ministry to their growing children. Perhaps God had that in mind when He said through the prophet Isaiah,

"Sing, O barren woman,
  you who never bore a child;
burst into song, shout for joy,
  you who were never in labor;
because more are the children of the
    desolate woman
  than of her who has a husband," says
    the Lord.

(Isaiah 54:1)

Pray for Your Children's Marriage Partners

Some years back we attended the marriage of Sharon Piper to Trent Thornton. (Trent and Sharon are now in their second term of Alliance missionary service in Hong Kong and expect to help lead the Alliance church-planting mission in the former Soviet Union.)

In the course of the ceremony, Sharon's father, Rev. James I. Piper, who was performing the ceremony, turned to the groom and said, "Sharon's mother and I have prayed for you since the day Sharon was born!"

Think of it. From the day they knew they had a daughter, the Pipers had been praying that God would send the right man to be Sharon's husband. And God abundantly answered.

Conclusion

God may or may not entrust you with material

wealth, or with many of the things that wealth makes possible. And if He should, you are well aware that you will not take any of it with you when you leave this earth (although it is possible to send some of it on ahead through your contributions to the Lord's work and to those in need). In fact, there is very little of a tangible nature that is transferrable at death. Not the home you live in. Not any of your material possessions. Not even your reputation and achievements, for only the saving blood of Jesus Christ can gain you access to heaven.

But if God has given you children, you not only have a benefit of inestimable worth in this life, but *one that you can take with you.* That priceless son or daughter, brought to faith in Christ through your prayers and godly instruction, the object of your parental love, can share all of eternity with you. What else here on earth even begins to match such a prospect? What in comparison is even remotely worth your effort?

When you stand before your Lord and Savior, will the circle be unbroken?

The two of us have had more than our share of blessings in life. A saving, sanctifying relationship with Jesus Christ ranks at the very top, of course. But there have been temporal blessings, too: friends, health, adequate income. Even a measure of acclaim. Those blessings, appreciated though they are, pale in comparison with another of transcending worth to us. Like the apostle John (3 John 4), we have no greater joy than to hear that our children are walking in the truth.

Rev. and Mrs. H. Robert Cowles are retired and live in Garner, North Carolina.

	Pray About
CHAPTER	**Church**
18	**Planting**
	by Steven C. Hammer

"MUCH PRAYER, MUCH POWER, LITTLE prayer, little power." Peter Deyneka's words arrested me the first time I read them. Not that power is the goal of prayer. Gene Edwards asks this rhetorical question in his book, *A Tale of Three Kings,* "What does this world need: Gifted men, outwardly empowered? Or broken men, inwardly transformed?" God's power at work through our broken lives is the only way anything eternal will be accomplished in this world. Therefore, it is essential that believers *pray about everything.* There are four factors which motivate us to do that in a society of self-sufficiency. We must revive the vision, regain the vitality, relate the value and restore the vulnerability of prayer.

Reviving the Vision for Prayer

A few years ago the Lancaster Christian and Missionary Alliance Church planted its first daughter congregation. Our long-range vision had always included church planting, but we had not expected to begin until later. We decided to construct our new building first.

Well, at least we thought we would. Instead, God was in the process of teaching us that vision for ministry must be held in an open hand. As we move forward in God's direction and as we seek Him in the place of prayer, He fine-tunes our vision. The one constant, however, in all that fine-tuning, is the vision for praying about everything, which sustains the church by maintaining an atmosphere of brokenness in the midst of change.

In our case those changes began with the realization that, even with multiple services and Sunday schools, the numerical growth of the church eventually would plateau before we could build. We had decided that one-third of the projected building cost would have to be on hand before breaking ground. Since we had just paid off our previous mortgage, built an expanded parking facility and prepared the site for the new building, we could not start right away.

An Adjusted Ministry Vision

In order to sustain growth we would have to adjust our ministry vision and plant a church as soon as possible. Then both mother and daughter churches would have room to grow. We could get back on the path to the original long-range vision soon enough. Through prayer and study we determined that the growing area of southern Lancaster County would be a good place to plant a church. We began to pray for 70–100 people who would be willing to commit themselves to starting a fellowship in this area.

We encouraged interested parties to meet during one of our Sunday school hours, and before long the group began to take shape. We held the group's tithes and offerings in escrow so the new church would be self-supporting from the start. We also appointed an advisory board and began meeting with the Eastern District Church Growth Director, Paul Sterneman, who encouraged us greatly. Also, the governing board had previously arranged for me to attend a Church Planter's Academy at Toccoa Falls College.

As the daughter church group gained momentum, we praised God for the mix of people He was drawing together. The prospect of giving to the new work such outstanding prayer warriors, church leaders, Christian educators, ministry coordinators, trained evangelists and musicians prompted us to say with King David, "[We] will not sacrifice to the Lord . . . offerings that cost [us] nothing" (2 Samuel 24:24).

Unanswered Questions

Many questions remained unanswered: Where would the new church meet? Who would be the pastor? What about a name? The people in our daily and weekly prayer meetings began holding up these needs to the Lord. In less than four months, 118 people met in a rented facility for the first service of the Countryside Christian and Missionary Alliance Church. A few weeks later, their fine pastor, Loren Salfrank, was in place. Both mother and daughter take to heart the challenge of Dennis Gorton, formerly of the Division of Church Ministries, who said, "We dream of 1,000 churches planting 1,000 churches. Dare we plant churches after our own kind if we are not praying churches? I envision 1,000 praying churches, empowered by God's Spirit, planting 1,000 praying churches." The very first church group began as a result of prayer. The Bible says of the early church, "They all joined together constantly in prayer" (Acts 1:14). The vision they started with, the vision to pray about everything, was the one constant that drove them as they held ministries with an open hand for God's fine-tuning along the way, fulfilling the Great Commission.

The anonymous author of the book, *The Kneeling Christian,* said, "God sometimes leads us into the prayer life. Sometimes, however, He has to drive us into such a life." In our self-sufficient society, God uses the vision for praying about everything to drive us back, again and again, to the place of prayer. That is a most blessed place to be, because He is the only One who can accomplish eternal tasks. And to think, He chooses to accomplish those tasks through His people who are broken before Him.

Regaining the Vitality for Prayer

"Each of my children is different." Perhaps most parents, at one time or another, have made such an assessment concerning their offspring. The same thing could be said by "mother" churches of their "offspring." We found that to be true as we experienced the birth of our latest daughter church.

In the early stages of the development of this new work, we kept waiting for the pieces of the puzzle to fall into place just as they did with our other "children." But this church plant did not seem to be working out the same way. The core group was struggling as a corporate entity.

When we began weekly meetings our goal was to start the church in approximately six months. Again, tithes and offerings were being held in escrow so that the church could be self-supporting when it began. We planned to have a full-time pastor in place from the start.

Setbacks

As the weeks passed, however, the number of interested people declined. Contributing to this, no doubt, was the fact that the mother church had just completed new worship and educational facilities. Additionally, some families were hesitant about moving their teenagers out of an established youth program.

The root of the problem, though, was much more serious. The old nemesis of prayerlessness had raised its head once again. It was not so much that we were not praying—we were. But our bent toward self-sufficiency was manifesting itself in a lack of intensity and fervency in prayer. In the words of Ron Hutchcraft, we were on "cruise control" concerning church planting.

Because we had become comfortable (if that is possible) in planting churches, God was allowing us to go through a time of frustration to deepen our dependence on Him. In his book, *Master Secrets of Prayer,* Cameron Thompson wrote: "Prayer is the spreading out of our helplessness . . . before the loving eyes of a Father who knows and understands and cares and answers. . . . *The secret of all failure is prayerlessness"* (emphasis added).

Renewal

As this need was expressed at one of our weekly early morning prayer meetings, we seemed to experience an immediate increase in our dependency upon God for the new church. We had new vitality! A few days later a pastor called to inquire about the work of The Alliance. As we met with him and God began to work, I wondered if he could be God's man for the new daughter church.

After a while, as we worked through district officials and core group leaders, the Lord confirmed that David Humphreville was supposed to be the new pastor. And the Lord used the news that a pastor had been found to give momentum to the church.

Then the rest of the puzzle pieces fell into place. By the target date, 35 adult charter members along with several adherents were commissioned as the Community Fellowship Church of The Christian and Missionary Alliance. The following Sunday, 91 persons attended the first service.

As God allows us to continue bearing fruit for Him by planting churches, we become more and more aware of our need for spiritual vitality. We thought we knew how to plant churches, but we discovered that we did not know what God had in mind for us.

It is only when we express an attitude of desperation in dependence upon God that we can assume a position where He is able to use us to accomplish His will.

As a mother church, we know that each one of our "children" may be different, but that is no problem for God. As in the case of our biological children, He has a unique plan and purpose for each one. And, as a side benefit, the mother church is allowed to grow in wisdom and faith along the way.

Relating the Value of Prayer

"This is just the beginning." "I am thirsty for more." "I wish we could continue past this week." These comments are typical of those made by people who attended our week of prayer.

Our people had been taking up the challenge to engage in spiritual warfare. We rejoiced together in Christ's victory on the cross and regularly applied that victory in our personal lives and in the church. Now, however, it seemed that the Lord wanted to teach us the value of corporate prayer in doing battle for Him.

This concept is reinforced by the "whole armor of God" motif, which concludes with these words: "And pray in the Spirit on all occasions with all kinds of prayers and requests. With this in mind, be alert and always keep on praying for all the saints" (Ephesians 6:18).

Planning for Prayer

The elders of the church spent several weeks praying for our week of prayer.

Preregistration was outstanding. We found that when people registered for the sessions ahead of time, they felt accountable for their participation. Preregistration also encouraged personal heart preparation. Of course, all sessions were open to everyone even if they had not registered.

The meetings were alive with God's manifest presence which allowed us the freedom to pray and testify. Devotional messages were especially outstanding.

Some who attended were new Christians who never before had prayed aloud in a group. What a blessing to speak with them afterward and learn that this had been one of the greatest experiences of their lives.

Because we had set aside evenings for prayer, we postponed all other adult ministries for a week. However, the youth of the church met for their regular evangelism ministry, which involved witnessing at a shopping mall.

Exciting Results

Our prayer meeting had just concluded when one of the youth teams burst through the doors of the church and reported that two teens contacted by the group had just made professions of faith in the Lord Jesus Christ. The young people's prayer partners in the church, some of whom are five times their age, rejoiced with them. Over the course of the week, there were 12 professions of faith reported.

Our week of prayer concluded with a testimony

service on Sunday evening. Many have spoken since then of a renewed boldness in their witnessing.

It has been said of a revival in Korea that when God broke through in answer to prayer, He did more in half a day than was accomplished by all missionary organizations in the previous six months under "normal" circumstances. According to the book, *The Kneeling Christian,* 2,000 were converted in less than two months at the outset of the revival.

We found setting a week of prayer to be worthwhile. In his sermon, "Fasting, Faith and Intercession," Keith Bailey states that "Prayer would be good for us even if we never got an answer to prayer."

People are finding themselves more and more in agreement with A.J. Gordon, who said, "We can do more than pray after we have prayed, but we can never do more than pray until we have prayed."

Someone else has said,

Why are many Christians defeated? Because they pray so little. Why do most people see so few brought out of darkness to light? Because they pray so little. Why are not our churches simply on fire for God? Because there is so little real prayer. All revivals have been the outcome of prayer.

We are trusting God to continue to bring into

focus the value of prayer as we attempt to impact our community with the gospel of the Lord Jesus Christ. We live in a relatively "religious" area. Yet surveys have concluded that many do not know for sure that they have eternal life. We need the quickening power of the Holy Spirit, not only to make Christ real to us but to awaken us to the spiritual needs all around us. This is just the beginning. We are thirsty for more.

Restoring the Vulnerability of Prayer

We, as a church, learned a little about vulnerability while preparing to build our new building. We found ourselves in the planning stage for approximately three years, and during most of that time we maintained a Sunday morning format of three worship services and two Sunday schools.

There were times when we wondered if the beginning of construction would ever take place. Three years is a long time to maintain momentum on a proposed building project, especially if there are no visible signs of progress (like a new building coming out of the ground).

If there is one lesson the Lord taught us during that time, it is the value of discipline. Sometimes it is so tempting to launch out on our own timetable and try to work things out in our own strength. Such efforts are futile. As Francis Schaeffer said in his sermon, "The Lord's Work in the Lord's Way":

The central problem of our age is not liberalism, modernism, the threat of communism or even the threat of rationalism and the monolithic consensus which surrounds us. All these are dangerous but not the primary threat. The real problem is this: the Church of the Lord Jesus Christ, individually or corporately, tending to do the Lord's work in the power of the flesh rather than of the Holy Spirit.

Disciplined Spending

We started out well. Our goal had been to build without debt. This is not a scriptural conviction with us but rather a desire to be fiscally responsible. We believe God desires for His people to exercise discipline in the way we spend money. We agree with Stephen F. Olford, who said at one of our leadership retreats, "God demands our tithes; He deserves our offerings; He defends our savings; and He directs our expenses."

We weren't able to reach our goal of building without debt. The willingness to be vulnerable and reach for a high goal was important, however, because we are in better shape fiscally than we would have been, had we not aimed so high.

There was an initial enthusiasm as we moved forward in this faith venture. However, the dynamics of working through the retirement of our previous mortgage, the construction of a new parking lot, and the improvement of our current educational and worship facilities (all part of our original master plan) contributed to an overall loss of momentum for the new building project.

Money from the Building Finance Program (BFP—a program sponsored by the Division of Church Ministries that enables churches to finance their building programs through faith pledges received over a three-year period) was going out for pre-approved projects just as fast as it was coming in. And it just is not exactly exciting to give toward debt retirement, parking lots and facility improvements.

Missing Enthusiasm

When all of the projects were completed and paid for, we found it difficult to regain our enthusiasm for giving toward the new building. We were tired of participating in the BFP. In addition, to sustain growth during a time of acute space problems, we planted that first daughter church, which meant giving up people from our church who were dedicated to doing the Lord's work.

We were thankful for God's hand moving among us in those ways, but we found ourselves languishing in a spiritual no-man's-land, where we were nearing the end of our three-year BFP and not one shovelful of dirt had been turned for our new building. We were hurting.

As we got down on our faces before God, He directed us to reapply some of the principles of the BFP. We called the church to prayer by forming several teams who participated in an all-church visitation over a three-week period. Immediately, we felt the effects of increased prayer. We began to regain momentum.

The momentum we gained through prayer caused us to gain momentum in all the other aspects of church life. A "Rekindling Our Vision" banquet was planned at a local restaurant. It was the best-attended function we have ever had outside the church. Ten-week financial commitments to the building fund were received at the banquet and during the following week.

Would We or Wouldn't We?

If the Lord allowed us to meet our goal for start-up money, we could break ground. If not, it was back to no-man's-land for a while. When the total of the financial commitments was announced, we found that we were far short of our goal. There was some disappointment, but we still had until midnight of the following Saturday for God to meet our need.

Prayer meetings that week were outstanding. Our Friday-night concert of prayer started slow but turned into one of the best we have ever had. When Saturday arrived without much improvement in the situation, it became a foregone conclusion that ground breaking would have to be pushed back—again.

At the Saturday night prayer meeting, we gave our concerns to God and went away with the peace that He was in control no matter how things turned out.

Eleventh Hour Victory

At 11:00 p.m., literally the 11th hour, I heard the news that God had broken through and all of the financial commitments needed for us to begin building were in place. In the last hour before the deadline, over $160,000 in financial commitments were received. This development reminded us, once again, of the trustworthiness of our living God.

According to my journal, the highlight of my devotional reading that Saturday was Isaiah 5:15–16: "So man will be brought low . . . but the LORD Almighty will be exalted." It has been said that failure is an event, not a person. Unless we are willing to fail, and that is the essence of vulnerability, we probably won't accomplish much for the Kingdom of God.

Peter Deyneka was right. There is much power that comes with much prayer. Therefore, believers should pray about everything. By doing so, we demonstrate brokenness in a self-sufficient society. Such a society is easy, even for professing Christians, to embrace unless we revive the vision for prayer, regain the vitality for prayer, relate the value of prayer and restore the vulnerability of prayer. After all, what does this world need: gifted men, outwardly empowered? or broken men, inwardly transformed?

Rev. Steven C. Hammer is the Senior Pastor of the Lancaster Alliance Church, Lancaster, Pennsylvania.

CHAPTER	Intercessory
19	Prayer

by Beverly Albrecht

IN A RECENT SUNDAY SCHOOL class I probed with this question: "How much time do you suppose the average Christian spends in prayer each day?" To my surprise, the consensus of the members was, "Maybe five minutes."

Yet on the other hand I am hearing worldwide reports of many individuals and even whole church denominations engaged in intercessory prayer. Peter Wagner, in his book *Warfare Prayer,* is convincing: "We're standing on the edge of what many believe is the greatest prayer movement of the 20th Century."

The need for prayer warriors is evident. Satan has mounted a massive attack against the church. Both abroad and at home, our Christian ranks have been thinned by wounded soldiers.

"Something strange is going on with your missionaries," a doctor said to an Alliance field director in a third-world country. He went on to explain that in a six-month time span four missionary women had consulted with him. Each was working with her husband in new, unchurched areas. All four women were having serious health problems; each was struggling to continue in her ministry. We hear similar reports from other areas of the world.

Satan seeks places of vulnerability for his most vicious attacks. Children of missionaries may have serious bouts of depression or mysterious headaches. Missionaries often hesitate to advise supporters about their own or their children's problems lest they be judged as ineffective. How vitally important it is to cover these "sent ones" with our prayers as they struggle against evil forces.

Some Still Are Unreached

Not only must we intercede for our front line troops, but there is an urgent call to pray for the remaining unreached people groups (UPGs) in our world today. (UPGs are distinguished by lingual, ethnic or geographic isolation; Christian believers in their number are practically non-existent.) God's heart is breaking for the lost peoples of our world. He sees vividly the total despair and darkness enveloping them.

We may tire of hearing about these unreached people. They seem remote and unrelated to our lives. But it is for these 11,000 remaining UPGs that we must pray if we are to bring back our King. Jesus said, " 'This gospel of the kingdom will be preached in the whole world as a testimony to all nations, and then the end will come' " (Matthew 24:14).

True intercession is threefold in nature. We must stand in the gap on behalf of others; we must demolish Satan's strongholds; we must ask for God's intervention in the affairs of mankind. We shall look at our role in all three—first to stand in the gap on behalf of others.

God Seeks Intercessors

The Lord declares: " 'I looked for a man . . . who would . . . stand before me in the gap on behalf of the land so I would not have to destroy it, but I found none. So I will pour out my wrath on them and consume them with my fiery anger, bringing down on their own heads all they have done' " (Ezekiel 22:30-31). Unless men and women are willing to intercede for those still in darkness, many will be destroyed.

Who is standing in the gap for the 30 million Islamic Sundanese of Indonesia? the Kabyles of Algeria? the Nuer of Sudan? Communism in the former Soviet Union has come crashing down because the heavenly vials of prayer overflowed. Now we must storm heaven's gates for the downfall of Islam. The One enthroned in heaven challenges His Son: " 'Ask of me,/and I will make the nations your inheritance,/the ends of the earth your possession' " (Psalm 2:8).

We can also stand in the gap for our fellow Christians who are experiencing attacks from the enemy. Remember how Jesus encouraged Peter when Satan was about to "sift [him] as wheat"? He said, " 'But I have prayed for you, Simon, that your faith may not fail' " (Luke 22:31-32).

A Personal Example

During our third year of missionary service in Indonesia, my husband, Wally, was hit by a very strange, sudden depression. It lasted two days and then, as suddenly, it lifted. Never before had he encountered anything like it. Ten days later he received a letter from a faithful praying friend.

"I know you're going through something you've never experienced before," his friend wrote with amazing prescience. "This thing that has come upon you is difficult to understand. I am praying for you that it will pass quickly." Wally rejoiced greatly to know that through this intercessor he had been granted quick deliverance, enabling him to continue unhindered in ministry.

Who will touch God's throne with one hand and reach out with the other to a weary missionary? Jesus says, " 'Ask and it will be given to you; seek and you will find; knock and the door will be opened to you' " (Luke 11:9).

Storming Satan's Strongholds

Second, as effective intercessors we can demolish the strongholds of Satan. "The weapons we fight with are not the weapons of the world. On the contrary, they have divine power to demolish strongholds. We demolish arguments and every pretension that sets itself up against the knowledge of God, and we take captive every thought to make it obedient to Christ" (2 Corinthians 10:4-5).

Jesus said to the 72 men He sent out into ministry, " 'I have given you authority to trample on snakes and scorpions and to overcome all the power of the enemy; nothing will harm you' " (Luke 10:19).

During the summer of 1991 our 16-year-old Megan had opportunity to serve with Youth With A Mission in Poland. Just before one of their public programs, they had gathered in groups of four to pray. Megan happened to notice a woman standing in the doorway of a nearby building. Upon seeing the woman, Megan was overcome by a strange fear. She shook uncontrollably.

Her partners wanted to know what was the matter. Megan shared the strange unease she felt about the woman standing a short distance from them. The group prayed that all fear would leave Megan and that she would be able to participate with the others. After the program, this same woman was sitting at a table, telling fortunes. Some of the group went over and began to pray fervently that her powers would be ineffective. And it was so! The woman, unable to proceed with her business, asked one of her friends to call the police to remove these prayer warriors who were hindering her witchcraft.

Spiritual Warfare and Prayer Go Together

It is important to understand that spiritual warfare and intercessory prayer are vitally linked together. Paul makes this clear to the Ephesian believers. He starts by saying: "God has . . . blessed us in the heavenly realms with every spiritual blessing in Christ" (1:3). Toward the end of the letter he advises them that "our struggle is not against flesh and blood, but against the rulers, against the authorities, against the powers of this dark world and against the spiritual forces of evil in the heavenly realms" (6:12). He concludes by adding, "Pray in the Spirit on all occasions with all kinds of prayers and requests. With this in mind, be alert and always keep on praying for all the saints" (6:18).

Paul links spiritual warfare and intercessory prayer. It is the task of the church to demolish the works of Satan by confronting the adversary with scriptural truth in prayer. God's "intent was that now, through the church, the manifold wisdom of God should be made known to the rulers and authorities in the heavenly realms according to his eternal purpose which he accomplished in Christ Jesus our Lord" (3:10).

We Must Resist Satan

To the Colossians Paul writes that Christ, "having disarmed the powers and authorities, . . . made a public spectacle of them, triumphing over them by the cross" (2:15). We must wage bold, aggressive prayer warfare in order to stand firm against the enemy's deception. The devil will always flee when we resist him (James 4:7).

We should not anticipate any letup. "The Spirit clearly says that in later times some will abandon the faith and follow deceiving spirits and things taught by demons" (1 Timothy 4:1).

To most Eastern minds, the spirit world is very real. Conversely, Western rationalism has had difficulty accepting the "authorities" and "powers" spoken of by Paul in Ephesians 6:12. But that has changed, as we are aware. The invasion of Eastern religions and the abandonment of biblical morality have brought an intense darkness to our North American world. The church is becoming conscious that indeed it is in a battle. There are forces to be confronted, and we had better not hide from the fact of their hideous existence. Once we as Christians admit to the reality of these forces, we can take up our weapons and do battle against them (2 Corinthians 10:4).

Confession Is Important

In her prayer seminar in Argentina, Cindy Jacobs

made a significant point. "When dealing with these strongholds of Satan," she said, "intercession alone will have little or no effect unless the underlying sins that allow Satan to rule are first dealt with."

All through the Scriptures we see the importance of confession of sins and repentance. Daniel repented for his people's sins, even though he himself may not have participated in them. He humbled himself, identifying with his fellow countrymen (Daniel 9:4-6). Nehemiah confessed the sins of his nation and of his father's house as he interceded for Israel (Nehemiah 1:5-7). Repentance and humility are powerful weapons that admit no counterattack.

In his book, *Taking Our Cities for God,* John Dawson tells how humility played an important role in disarming the forces of evil. He and others were attempting to reach the city of Cordoba, Argentina, for Christ. They had had little success in their witness. Finally they realized they were dealing with a spirit of pride. God revealed to them that they should kneel in humility as they prayed in the streets and fashionable shopping malls. Immediately the Lord began to work, and people came forward to receive Christ. The weapons we wield are powerful, provided they are not tainted by worldly glamor or pride.

Ask for Divine Intervention

Third, we can become effective intercessors by asking for God's intervention in the affairs of mankind.

When Pharaoh and his army threatened to annihilate Israel at the Red Sea, Moses cried out to the Lord for His intervention. Almost at once "the angel of God, who had been traveling in front of Israel's army, withdrew and went behind them [as protection against the pursuers]" (Exodus 14:19). Hezekiah cried out to the Lord for His intervention against Sennacherib and his army. That very night, the Lord sent His angel to destroy 185,000 of the Assyrian army (2 Kings 19:9-36). How awesome to see God's immediate response to these prayers for help!

When the early church fervently interceded for Peter, who had been imprisoned, God intervened, sending an angel to release Peter from the chains and bars restricting him. Peter was able to show himself to all those who were praying for him (Acts 12:1-19).

We Have Many Models

God intends His church to be a strong, triumphant body. We should visualize ourselves as bold, aggressive prayer warriors. The Scriptures give us many models of intercessors who turned the direction of history through their prayers: Abraham, Moses, Elijah, Jehoshaphat, Daniel—to name a few of the more prominent ones. Jesus Himself interceded for His disciples and for those who would later believe through their witness (John 17). One of His continuing occupations is intercession (Hebrews 7:25).

These prayed boldly, believingly, persistently. God honors such praying. Indeed, He commands us to pray that way. We must not see ourselves as limp, lazy losers, but as victorious soldiers in the heavenly battle.

When we intercede for others we generate large amounts of spiritual energy, love, support, protection and encouragement. People's lives are changed. Nations are spared. Those living in darkness are freed from the evil controlling them.

Perhaps a Prayer Room?

It would do us well to establish a prayer room in every church possible. For those too timid to pray in public, the privacy of a prayer room where just two or three people might meet together can be an ideal spot for fervent intercessory prayer.

The requests may cover a host of needs local, national and worldwide. Requests from our missionaries can be pored over, providing a continuous cover for these representatives as they minister in difficult places.

Housewives who sense a special calling to get involved in intercessory prayer can form home prayer cells. Retired people may be willing to devote lengthy periods of time to prayer. Like the prophets of old, all of these can have a telling impact in the heavenly realms where the strategic battle continues.

Conclusion

God is calling a great host of intercessors—people who long to see evil exposed and demolished, who long to see Satanic strongholds crumble, who long to see people turn to the Savior. We are believing God for a great revival in His church. Admittedly, the darkness is intense. Evil influence is growing at an alarming rate. Opposition to evangelical Christian faith is increasing. But God has His time for harvest. He wants many prayer warriors to claim His promises and get involved. He calls us to use this mighty weapon He has given us.

Nothing can be more important than the fulfillment of this high calling. "The eyes of the Lord are on the righteous, / and his ears are attentive to their cry" (Psalm 34:15). Let us not exchange our divine armor for a comfortable robe. With joy and perseverance let us become actively involved in intercessory prayer.

The work of Christ's kingdom depends on it.

Mrs. Beverly Albrecht serves with her husband Wally, Director of Missions and Personnel, at the Canadian National Office of The Christian and Missionary Alliance in Canada.

Prayer for the Churches

by Dahl B. Seckinger

WHY LIVE ON WELFARE WHEN you can be a millionaire? God has provided unlimited resources for us!

Most parents think of the potential residing in their children and desire them to be all they were created to be. Paul's prayer in Ephesians 3:14–21 reminds us that our Heavenly Father also longs to see His children live their spiritual lives to the full, drawing from His abundant riches:

For this reason I kneel before the Father, from whom his whole family in heaven and on earth derives its name. I pray that out of his glorious riches he may strengthen you with power through his Spirit in your inner being, so that Christ may dwell in your hearts through faith. And I pray that you, being rooted and established in love, may have power, together with all the saints, to grasp how wide and long and high and deep is the love of Christ, and to know this love that surpasses knowledge—that you may be filled to the measure of all the fullness of God.

Now to him who is able to do immeasurably more than all we ask or imagine, according to his power that is at work within us, to him be glory in the church and in Christ Jesus throughout all generations, for ever and ever! Amen.

Preparation—Ephesians

The above prayer is the second of two in this relatively short letter to the Ephesian Christians. The first (1:15–23) expresses Paul's desire that these believers be enlightened as to their potential in Christ Jesus. This second prayer deals with God's power available to them to reach that potential.

Historically, the letter has been considered as directed to the church in Ephesus. But some early manuscripts lack the words *in Ephesus*. This omission and Paul's use of the phrase, "To the . . . faithful in Christ Jesus" (1:1) suggest that we may apply the letter to all who are "faithful in Christ Jesus"—including present-day believers. Paul is concerned that Christians grasp all of God's provision for them. He wants us to understand that we may appropriate His life and riches in our everyday experience.

Because of his preaching, Paul was confined in Rome, chained to a guard. He made that prison his preaching point, his prayer room and a place to model the sufficiency of Christ's indwelling life. Amid personal poverty he experienced inner richness. At a time when he had ample reason to despair, he wrote with hope. Although his circumstances dictated limits, he magnified a God able and willing to do more than he could ask or think. His prayer for the Ephesians strains human language to express the fullness of Christ he has experienced and that God yearns to provide for all His children.

Why not pray this prayer personally as we explore its richness? Why not ask God to help you understand and appropriate God's abundant provision "out of his riches" for your own life? Then determine to live your life drawing on God's presence and power.

What Prompted Paul to Pray this Way?

It is obvious that an important message precedes this prayer in chapter 3. Something has propelled Paul into his outburst of superlatives: "glorious riches," "love that surpasses knowledge," "all the fullness of God," "immeasurably more than all we ask or imagine."

Earlier Paul has detailed the past lives of the Ephesians—indeed, of all who are outside of Christ. He calls them transgressors dead in their sins, disobedient, living in darkness. He says they followed the cravings of their sinful nature, invoking God's wrath. They were separated from Christ Jesus, excluded from citizenship in God's Israel, foreigners to God's covenants of promise. They were without hope, without place, without God.

"But now," because of God's great love and mercy, they have been forgiven, have been made alive in Christ, have been brought near to God. "But now" they are fellow citizens with God's people, members of God's household, part of that one body of Christ, sharers together in the promises in Jesus Christ. He even reminds them that they are being built together to become a dwelling in which God lives by His Spirit (see chapter 2).

We Should Not Be Surprised

Are we surprised that Paul, overwhelmed by the magnificent work of God in the lives of these first century believers should "kneel before the Father, from whom his whole family in heaven and on earth derives its name," overwhelmed in wonder, awe and adoration? Even his posture denotes humility as he proclaims the fact that salvation and sufficiency have been provided by a loving Father God for spiritual children encompassing the universe!

And from that group of believers in Ephesus, down through the corridors of church history, Paul moves to you and me today and to all who will yet accept and experience the life of God. He declares all of us "fellow citizens with God's people and members of God's household, built on the foundation of the apostles and prophets, with Christ Jesus himself as the chief cornerstone. In him the whole building is joined together and rises to become a holy temple in the Lord" (2:19–22).

Can you imagine the scene? I can visualize a husky Roman soldier beside Paul, possibly having to kneel also because the two men were chained to each other, listening to this prayer. I wonder if that soldier, as he heard Paul's words about freedom, love and fullness in Christ Jesus, may have been among those of Caesar's household who came to faith in Jesus Christ (Philippians 4:22).

Paul leads us up a mental stairway, from landing to landing, opening door after door, to reveal the great spiritual vistas that are ours to claim in Christ Jesus. We come as children to our Father with every confidence that what He has promised He will provide. He is our Father, full of grace and truth. He does not withhold any good thing from us, His beloved children. As we peruse this prayer, we bow together with Paul in gratitude and adoration.

The Prayer Itself

Paul makes three separate requests in his prayer in Ephesians 3:16–21. The three are linked together like a chain, leading us toward a great crescendo of praise to God. They reveal the very essence of God's purposes: "glory in the church and in Christ Jesus throughout all generations, forever and ever."

Paul prays that (1) God "out of his glorious riches . . . may strengthen you with power through his Spirit in your inner being, so that Christ may dwell in your hearts through faith;" (2) that "you, being rooted and established in love, may have power, together with all the saints, to grasp how wide and long and high and deep is the love of Christ;" and (3) that you will "know this love that surpasses knowledge—that you may be filled to the measure of all the fullness of God."

Those provisions of God's abundance that Paul longed for the believers of his day to experience, God is still offering today to us, His children.

"Strengthened with Power" (3:16)

The presence of the Holy Spirit in us seals our salvation. But Paul was praying for something more. He wanted the Ephesians to have a new understanding of the practical implications of the Spirit's power and work in their lives in an ongoing way. The Spirit's power in their inner being would enable them to live lives that were Christlike and Christ-centered. Paul opened a whole treasure house of possibilities. He says that God strengthens us according to His glorious riches. God's power is not limited to our expectations or resources.

Multimillionaire Henry Ford was known for his practice of giving away dimes he always had in his pocket. He gave sparingly from his riches! But God gives abundantly from His inexhaustible resources. Paul assured the Ephesians of abundant strength from the God who gives freely. Before salvation, the Ephesians were, in Paul's words "dead in your transgressions and sins" (2:1). None of us can live a Christ-centered life by ourselves. But we have a power Source and a Control Center when the Holy Spirit enlivens our dead spirits.

God's Holy Spirit in our lives is the executor of the Father's wealth of power. This is inner power: not a surge of power that brings an occasional spurt of energy, but ongoing, never-ending, inexhaustible power that enables us, despite our weakness, to live our lives in God's strength. *Dwell* is a word of permanence. It means to take up residence. It connotes finality. God is saying, "This is the place where I have chosen to live, to stay."

"So that Christ may dwell in your hearts through faith." As we understand this great truth and yield full ownership of our lives to the indwelling Christ, we can know the reality expressed by Alfred C. Snead in his hymn, "Fully Surrendered":

Fully surrendered—life, time and all,
All Thou hast given me held at Thy call.
  Speak but the word to me,

> Gladly I'll follow Thee,
> Now and eternally
>   Obey my Lord.

"Rooted and Established in Love" (3:17–18)

When Christ is dwelling in our hearts, we become "rooted and established" in His love.

Rooted brings word pictures to our minds. We think of gigantic trees whose roots go deep into the earth, firmly holding the trunk and branches in wind and storm. Roots bring nourishment as well as strength. They transfer nutrients and water, enabling the tree to flourish, to become productive, to offer shade and shelter. It is impossible for a tree to grow without roots, but the soil is important too. The soil, says Paul, is God's love. We are rooted in God's love. He is the very Source of our lives.

Established is a builder's term. A contractor who builds a house must have a good foundation. One of the churches in which I ministered had the joy of constructing a new building. But we could not build where we originally intended. We needed a place that offered a firmer foundation.

The foundation is the most critical part of a building. Jesus told a story about two builders: one who built on rock and one who built on sand (Matthew 7:24–29). The wind and water destroyed the house with the poor foundation. It was not "established." It was not settled securely, was not fixed in a stable condition.

Paul notes that our foundation is God's love. He reminds us that our security is in God's everlasting love for us. God so loved us that he gave His Son; Christ Jesus so loved us that He died for our sins.

Human love has limitations. It may be fickle and temporary, depending on the response of the other person. Paul's prayer takes us beyond ourselves! He prays that we will "grasp" (take in our hands) and "know" (apprehend, make it our own) God's love in all its dimensions. He prays that we will really know how wide and long and high and deep the love of Christ is.

We Are Finite in Our Understanding

What does *wide* mean to you? East to west? God loves us so much that He has separated our sins from us "as far as the east is from the west" (Psalm 103:12). How wide is wide?

How long is *long*? " 'I have loved you with an everlasting love,' " God says through Jeremiah (31:3). There is no end to God's love. It goes on and on, forever and ever.

How high is *high*? When we think of "high," we look at the moon, the stars, the heavens. There seems to be no ceiling. The psalmist declares to God, "Great is your love, higher than the heavens; / your faithfulness reaches to the skies" (108:4).

How deep is *deep*? When I think of "deep," I visualize the ocean depths, but the ocean has a bottom. Song writers avow that God's love "reaches to the lowest hell," seeking to restore lost sinners far off from God. How can we understand the deep love of God? Samuel T. Francis wrote:

Oh, the deep, deep love of Jesus,
 Vast, unmeasured, boundless, free;
Rolling as a mighty ocean
 In its fullness over me.
Underneath me, all around me,
 Is the current of Thy love;
Leading onward, leading homeward,
 To my glorious rest above.

A Paradox

What Paul expresses is a paradox. He prays that we will know the love of God which passes knowledge! It is like the "unsearchable" riches in Christ about which Paul preached to the Gentiles (Ephesians 3:8). We never have to worry about God's running out of the spiritual resources we need for our Christian lives! God also wants us to understand that we can give to others out of our overflowing supply—"filled to the measure of all the fullness of God" (3:19).

How can you add a superlative to a superlative? Paul here is expressing abundance beyond our comprehension. God wants us to live in His fullness. There are two parts to this fullness, the positional and the practical. When we come to know Christ as Savior, we are made complete in Him (Colossians 2:9). We are full; there is nothing more that needs to be accomplished to become a child of God. He has provided it all.

There is, however, a practical, everyday working out of this fullness. Paul reminds us that we are to "work out [our] salvation" (Philippians 2:12). In other words, we need to appropriate God's fullness as our own in daily life. Practically, we live in the love of Christ only to the measure of our comprehension of that love. We must apply the resources and power of God. And, obviously, if we are to be filled, we must first be emptied. I must yield myself to His love and life.

"Filled to the Measure of All the Fullness of God" (3:19)

Can there be anything more? As if we did not totally understand the God to whom Paul is praying, he concludes with a magnificent picture of an all-sufficient Father: "Now to him who is able to do immeasurably more than all we ask or imagine, according to his power that is at work within us, to him be glory in the church and in Christ Jesus throughout all generations forever and ever. Amen.

Why live on welfare when you can be a millionaire? Why live in your own poverty when Christ's plan is to share Himself and His riches with you? Let it never be said of you or me, "You have not because you ask not" (James 4:2).

> Thou art coming to a King,
> Large petitions with thee bring;
> For His grace and pow'r are such,
> None can ever ask too much.
> John Newton

Rev. Dahl B. Seckinger is the superintendent of the Great Lakes District, Ann Arbor, Michigan.

Let's Have Revival Now. What Are We Waiting For?

CHAPTER
21

A serious call
to revival in our
churches—*now.*

by Armin Gesswein

W E ARE LIVING IN CRESCENDO times—full of quick changes and new challenges—the "last days." Days when "evil men and imposters go from bad to worse, deceiving and being deceived" (2 Timothy 3:13).

Days when God is also at work as never before.

There is only one throne, and Jesus is on it—not the devil. And He is not playing catch-up on the devil either! It's the other way, but it takes watchful eyes to see that.

For one thing, there is now a whole new wave of prayer in our land: prayer conferences, concerts of prayer, prayer rallies and prayer seminars. Entire denominations have been shaping up for a whole "year of prayer." May it all increase with the increase of God!

Nothing, I suppose, is more prayed about, or more needed, than revival. And nothing is more promised in Scripture. Yet no praying seems to be so little answered.

Most of the praying sounds as if revival is always "going to be." We constantly hear the phrase "when revival comes."

But when? We don't expect it *now*.

And so we futurize and generalize and procrastinate it!

Praying for revival is not the same as revival-praying.

Our land has never been more needy, and God knows it calls for a spiritual revival. But while we keep sending up petitions for our land, Jesus is saying what about your churches?

Revival is for God's people. It is not a call to the White House, but to God's house. We want a landslide while we let our churches backslide. It's like praying for a forest fire to get our fireplaces going! We say revival is all in God's hand while we let our prayer meetings get out of hand and die.

My subject is: *Let's Have Revival Now. What Are We Waiting For?*

—"Now is the time of God's favor . . . (2 Corinthians 6:2); —"Today, if you hear his voice, / do not harden your hearts" (Hebrews 3:15); —"He who has an ear, let him hear what the Spirit says to the churches" (Revelation 2:7).

The book of Hebrews warns against hardness of heart, and the book of Revelation warns against being hard of hearing.

In Revelation chapter 1, the Lord is blasting a trumpet so loudly that all of the seven churches (meaning any and every church) are to hear it, wake up, repent, be revived and get on fire for God. Then as if that were not enough, He lifts up His voice with the roar of a Niagara with the same message, while He walks in the midst of those churches. Finally, the Holy Spirit also penetrates our eardrums seven times with the same words to every one of those seven churches: "He who has an ear, let him hear what the Spirit says to the churches."

Think of it! All these are siren-like voices, and we pay little or no attention to them. We don't even seem to hear them!

And so we wait for Christ's second coming to take us out of a miserable world, while He is blasting his trumpet for us to wake up, get our churches wakened up and on fire for God in this miserable world!

Are we waiting for the coming of the Lord to do what the coming of His Spirit wants to do now?

The coming of the Holy Spirit with power in our churches is not only needed for the evangelizing of the world—it also is the best preparation for the coming of the Lord. Nothing makes us more ready for heaven than living in the "heavenlies" now. The message on the coming rapture is never more wonderful than in a revival of the church.

Question: Is the Lord going to forget all about the backsliding in these churches and simply sweep them all into glory at any moment?

Here He is calling them to repent and get back to the glory they have lost.

When Jesus ascended to heaven, the Holy Spirit descended upon His church—and when He descends again, His church will ascend— prepared as a bride to meet the Bridegroom. The cloud of glory which attended His ascension is to rest upon our churches. His bride will never be more ready for the rapture than when she is enraptured by His Spirit in her "first love" (Revelation 2:4). In the Revelation, it is the Spirit and the bride who say "Come!" (Revelation 22:17, 20).

Question: Do we really mean it when we say we want revival?

Various reasons are given for not having revival in our churches now. Some even say that the "prophetic Scriptures" tell us we are now in the "last days"—days of "the apostasy" and "falling away from the faith" . . . like in the days of Noah and Sodom and Gomorrah—which are against expecting to see revival now. "Prophecy," they tell us, is against it.

But the book of Revelation is prophecy! That's all it is, all the way through. Full, final, authentic biblical prophecy! In it God is prophetically blowing His trumpet to get His preachers and churches to wake up spiritually, repent and get back to their original power from on high and wake up their cities for God.

Isn't is strange how we can postpone revival, or express doubt about it while we keep on praying for it? We even use "prophecy" to put off the very thing it is calling us to do!

What is it we are postponing?

We are postponing our priorities.

We are postponing our prayerfulness.

We are postponing our repentance.

God is speaking as loudly as He can—but we do not listen.

The fact is, most of the reasons advanced for not having revival in our churches are the very reasons for it. They are just another way of expressing our fallen condition. These prophetic messages of Revelation are God's call to revival—not against it!

The devil is very tricky and busy with all kinds of doubts and delay tactics. He is a master of doubt, delay, deceit and denial. He hates revival and is its number one enemy. His voices are many, but God's voice is one—always the same seven times: "He who has an ear, let him hear what the Spirit says to the churches."

Question: Are we clear about what we mean by "revival"? What are we looking for? From where do we expect it to come? When? How?

Revival, we know, is a church word: Reviving those who have life in Christ. The New Testament is never vague or general about it. We are always thinking revival in our land; in the New Testament God is calling to revival in our needy churches. God does not call us to some kind of a future revival; He calls for church revivals now.

Pentecost was a church revival and launched us into God's New Age—an age to be characterized by church revivals.

Revival is God's answer to the New Age Movement. Pentecost sets the pattern and the pace for church revivals.

Jesus never said anything more plainly: ". . . I will build my church, and the gates of Hades will not overcome it" (Matthew 16:18). A more powerful word never hit the ether waves.

The big question remains: How?

How would He do this? What did He build?

Would you believe it? He built a prayer meeting (Acts 1). The Acts then becomes the story of that prayer meeting. It quickly becomes His new church, always advancing as it began, by prayer.

That little church is not only the mother of churches—it is the model. Clear as this is, churches miss it for the most part.

This church gives us the Bible basis for church prayer meetings. Most churches don't seem to know this and miss it.

It also gives us the much needed Bible basis for expecting church renewal, church awakenings, church revivals. And by "church" I mean "congregation" (the meaning of the word *ecclesia* here).

Knowing this, we can pray expecting the Lord to give us strong prayer meetings and powerful congregational revivals.

The church . . . the church . . . the church. That's where the rubber continues to meet the road all through the New Testament.

On one day alone—the day of Pentecost—about 3,000 Jews were converted to the Messiah and were added to this new church. That's a manifestation of power from on high the like of which was never known before! After that, we are told, the Lord continued to add to that number daily "those who were being saved" (Acts 2:47).

On and on the story goes like that, as this church becomes the centerpiece of history, turning it into His Story!

The Apostle Paul did not breeze through country after country with the gospel. He planted churches everywhere. He followed that up with his famous epistles—letters to many of those churches—in Thessalonica, Corinth, Galatia, Philippi, Colossians, Ephesus and Rome.

Question: How are we to take our cities for God? That's a big question today.

Paul's method was to get his churches on fire for Christ—the same plan the Lord modeled with His first church in Jerusalem. That plan—church awakenings and revivals—has always been God's way in all the great revivals. It was the plan in the Norway revivals, where I ministered. It was the plan in the Wales revival. It certainly was the plan in all the many revivals under Charles G. Finney. He had no other plan. And his track record is one of the greatest of his century. Sometimes a whole city was awakened and turned to the Lord. How did he do it? He got the churches awakened to pray, and then in that atmosphere he preached his powerful messages of repentance. Like the Jerusalem church, he got the churches on fire—so strongly that he did not have to chase all the devils out of town! The churches were too hot for the devil and he "beat it!" At least for a while.

So we see, in the New Testament, the local congregation keeps getting the call to revival. It is the major unit for the mighty working of the Holy Spirit.

The book of Revelation is God's final Amen for this. It knows no other vision of revival and sounds out the last call to revival in the New Testament. It is also the loudest. He literally trumpet blasts the call to the churches to repent, be revived and return to their "first love" and do again "the things [they] did at first" (Revelation 2:5).

There should never be any doubt in any preacher's mind, or in anybody else's, that congregational revival is serious business.

But when? That is the final question. When will the revival come to the ministers and their churches?

God wants it now!

No waiting—except waiting on the Lord in prayer and following through with Him. For He is the real Revivalist in the midst of His churches. " 'Not by might, nor by power, but by my Spirit,' says the LORD Almighty" (Zechariah 4:6).

There is a lot of praying about revival, but that will not bring it about! Jesus did not pray about things—He brought them about by prayer.

Revival must be birthed—prayed into being, just as Pentecost was born in the famous Upper Room "constantly in prayer" (Acts 1:14).

Dr. A.T. Pierson said it well, when he said that no revival has ever come except by that kind of praying, and (he continued) no revival has ever continued beyond the continuation of the same kind of praying. *It's like a fire: what gets it started is what it takes to keep it burning.*

Let's gather the elders. The leaders. The like-minded. Build the broken altars. The broken prayer altars. The broken family altars. The broken-down prayer meetings. We must pursue. Persevere. Pray through. Follow Him through . . . to revival in our churches . . . now!

Rev. Armin Gesswein, a long-time Alliance minister, serves as Founder and Director of The Revival Prayer Fellowship, Inc., and the Ministers' Prayer Fellowship.

How to Develop a Private Prayer Life

CHAPTER

22

by Richard M. Sipley

WHEN IT COMES TO BREATH-
ING, either you breathe or you
are dead. For the Christian, prayer is no less essential. Either you pray or you are dead. Prayer is just
that important.

At one time or another, all true Christians have
desired to develop a private prayer life. New
believers are most open to the possibility because
they recognize their need. But over the years their
lives fill up with many other activities, and slowly
they give up on prayer.

Other factors militate against establishing and
maintaining a private prayer life. Some Christians
may never have been taught how to pray. Or they
may have been unwilling to pay the full price of
devotion to God. Whatever the reason, it is ex-
tremely sad to realize that many so-called Chris-

tians live out their entire lives—20, 40, 60 years—without developing a real life of private prayer. Little wonder so many church members live in total defeat and even question the Christian life.

Moody Learned the Value of Prayer

Early in his ministry, shortly after the Chicago fire from which his church was trying to recover, Dwight L. Moody decided to make a trip to London to listen to Charles H. Spurgeon and other pulpit masters. While there he agreed to an impromptu invitation from a minister to preach the next Sunday morning and evening to his congregation.

It was a large church, Moody said, and it was full. But he found it hard going to preach. The people looked to be carved out of stone—and just as responsive. By the time he was half through, he wished he was not there. And he wished just as heartily that he had not promised to return that evening.

Moody spent the afternoon in prayer. And at the appointed hour, he was back. Again he faced a packed church. Again his audience was respectful, quiet, attentive, but very cold. As he struggled in his preaching, suddenly it was as if someone had opened a door, allowing God's heavenly breeze to enter. Everything changed. The people changed. The whole atmosphere changed. *Moody changed.* He sensed the anointing of the Holy Spirit and he began to preach with great liberty and unction.

As he concluded his message, Moody felt compelled to extend an invitation to anyone interested in becoming a Christian. To his amazement, people began standing all over the audience. Certain that he had been misunderstood, Moody re-phrased the invitation. Again there was the same overwhelming response. Moody ministered there for ten days, during which time 400 people were soundly converted and added to the church. Every church within a ten-mile radius was greatly moved in that outpouring of the Holy Spirit. For Moody it was the launch of one of the greatest evangelistic careers the church of Jesus Christ has seen.

Meanwhile, Behind the Scene . . .

How does that anecdote fit the theme of this chapter? Moody realized that the remarkable outpouring of God's Spirit had nothing to do with him. So he searched for its cause. He learned that there was a woman in that congregation, bedfast because of a lingering illness, who had given herself to private prayer. Daily she spent many hours in intercession, asking God to pour out His Spirit to save the lost and revive His people.

One day there came into her hands a magazine containing a printed sermon by a Chicago preacher, Dwight L. Moody. She had never heard his name, but her heart burned as she read the sermon. She began to pray that God would bring Mr. Moody to her church.

This woman lived with an able-bodied sister who attended the church regularly. One Sunday noon, the sister returned home to announce that a Mr. Dwight Moody had preached at church that morning and would be speaking again in the evening. The bedfast woman blanched in surprise. She refused dinner, saying she would spend the afternoon in prayer. That evening, as the service was in progress, she went up that last steep hill of prayer and claimed Satan's citadel. The outcome was incalculable.

This life of private prayer is more important than any other thing that is done by anyone in the kingdom of God. No other ministry has as great an impact as prayer.

A Five-Point Outline

In the first half of Luke 11, the evangelist reports some of Jesus' important teaching on prayer. His disciples had watched Jesus pray, had been with Him when He prayed, had seen the impact of His praying on their lives. Now they turned to Him with their request: "Lord, teach us to pray."

So Jesus gave them a simple method—simple, but by no means easy—by which they could develop a personal prayer life of their own. Here are Jesus' five points:

- Pray routinely (11:2-4)
- Pray persistently (11:5-8)
- Pray specifically (11:9-13)

- Pray authoritatively (11:14-26)
- Pray regularly (11:1-2)

We shall look at them in this order, reserving the very beginning of the chapter for the last.

Pray Routinely

The word may strike you as strange, but I know of no other, for this is exactly what I mean. There are some things a Christian should be praying about on a routine basis. I know that can be boring. And I know there have been all kinds of neat books written about making prayer exciting, but if they deny what I am saying here, please disregard them. There is no way around the fact that prayer is a discipline of the Christian life.

But exactly what do I mean by "routinely?" I mean just what Jesus set before His disciples. " 'When you pray, say . . . ' "—and then He gave them what we commonly call the Lord's Prayer. Do I mean we should say the Lord's Prayer every time we pray? Certainly not! But I think we need to pray through some things every time we come apart for private prayer.

How I Pray Routinely

Each morning when I pray I start out by worshiping God. "Father, hallowed [holy] be Your name." Isn't that a good place to start? I worship God. I praise Him. I tell Him I love Him. I thank Him for keeping me and my family throughout the night. I thank Him for His grace and love to me. And usually there is something special I can thank Him for.

Then I pray for the coming of God's kingdom. I ask God to cleanse me from sin for my participation in His kingdom work that day. I ask Him to do the same for my wife. And I ask God to fill us both to overflowing with His Spirit for the kingdom ministries before us. I ask Him for power. I ask Him for the gifts we will need throughout the day.

From there I branch out to our children and what is going on in their lives. I pray that God will make them what He wants them to be. I go over their lives and pray for them. I do the same for brothers and sisters. I pray for our church and the members of its pastoral staff. I pray for the governing board. I pray for the membership, for the various departments of the church.

"But," you ask, "doesn't all that get boring?" Yes, it does.

"Then why do you keep it up?"

Because I'm supposed to. And that's the way to do it. Routine praying—things we need to pray about on a daily basis because they are daily needs.

Pray Persistently

Then you also need to pray persistently. That means to pray for some things over and over, keeping them before God until He gives you a final answer. There are two ways you can get a final answer when you are praying persistently. God may indicate to you in your spirit that He has answered that prayer and that you don't have to pray about the matter any more. Or God may indicate to you that He will *not* do anything about that matter because . . . . That kind of an answer scares me and upsets me. It means someone has rebelled against God to the point of no return.

With most of our persistent prayers, we pray until we see the answer or have the assurance that God is going to answer. You will recall Paul's prayers for his "thorn". He asked God to remove the thorn. No answer. He asked again and yet again. God answered, but not in the way Paul anticipated. God promised sufficient grace to bear the trial.

Sometimes I wonder how many wonderful answers we miss because we do not persist. As a pastor I am frequently asked to stand with someone in prayer about a certain matter. I am saddened when, though I know in my spirit that it's not time to quit, the other person gets discouraged and gives up. Don't quit too soon! Persist and pray through!

Pray Specifically

Next, Jesus talked to His disciples about specific praying. They were to ask specifically—for fish, if that was the need, or for an egg. And when they asked, they could expect a specific answer. God would not instead send them a snake or a scorpion.

Praying specifically is to pray carefully. Think through what you want from God. When Jesus asked the blind beggar, " 'What do you want me to do for you?' " (Luke 18:41), the man was very specific: " 'Lord, I want to see.' "

We need to decide what we want from God, and then we need to pray for that thing or those things. Ask, seek, knock were Jesus' instructions as He talked to His disciples about prayer (11:9). We ask with our mouths and voices, confessing our specific need. We seek with our eyes—seeking is a visual exercise. In prayer, we need to visualize in our minds what we are asking for with our mouths. Sometimes we ask God for one thing but visualize a different thing. That doesn't work. Knocking is an action word. We do what God says to do. We obey His orders. We follow Him, wherever He leads.

Confession, vision, action. There is confession with the mouth, there is vision in the heart and mind, and there is action of the life in obedience to God. That is specific praying.

Pray Authoritatively

Then we need to pray authoritatively. More and more I am convinced that in this day in which we live here in North America we Christians must do more warfare praying than we currently do. Things are happening in the lives of Christians and non-Christians that can be attributed directly to the influence of demonic powers. That general statement is hardly a surprise to us. But when in our private prayer lives we pray for a person, does it cross our minds that the person we are praying for may be under the power of Satan and in need of some definite warfare praying for his or her release?

You ask, "What is 'warfare praying'?" Let me answer by telling you how it works for me.

God lays a person or a situation upon my heart. I take that one or that thing to Him in private prayer. But as I pray day after day, I come to a point where I sense I am getting nowhere. So I ask God, "Lord, tell me—speak to my heart—is there anything demonic in this situation? Is the enemy involved in any way?"

No Known Sin

Follow carefully here, because this is something you do not want to do carelessly. If I sense God calling me to pray about demonic activity, I first make sure that I have confessed every known sin and that I am washed clean in the blood of Jesus. I ask God to cover me and my family and all that pertains to me with Jesus' blood. Next I claim Jesus' promise to His disciples (you and I are His disciples, too): " 'I have given you authority . . . to overcome all the power of the enemy; nothing will harm you' " (Luke 10:19).

Then I address Satan and those evil spirits: "*In the name of Jesus* I bind you. I command every one of you who has anything to do with this person or this situation to leave and to go to your own place." I may repeat that process for a number of days or weeks. Exorcising evil spirits can take time. But as I continue to put pressure on these evil powers, I begin to notice things starting to happen. The person or the situation begins to free up, or the devil manifests himself in some way so that he is out in the open where he can be dealt with.

Our all-powerful God can bring deliverance and freedom to people, situations and problems all around us. In our private times with God we need to do some warfare praying. But again a word of caution: It is absolutely essential that we keep our own lives clean before God. Sinless? None of us is. But if we confess our sins, God is ready to forgive and cleanse us so that we are in a position to pray in Jesus' name and with His authority—and His results.

Pray Regularly

Fifth and last, we are to pray regularly. If we will be honest, that is hardest of all, isn't it? I wonder if there has ever been a Christian who never had a problem about praying regularly. Do I have a problem about praying regularly? Absolutely!

Pray regularly. How, you wonder, do I get that idea out of the first two verses of Luke 11? Luke tells us, "One day Jesus was praying in a certain place." As you read the Gospels, you discover they are saturated with statements about Jesus' praying. They speak about His arising early in the morning to pray, about His finding a solitary place to pray, about His praying all night. You have to be convinced that prayer was a habit of Jesus' life. Prayer was His regular practice. Moreover, Jesus began His instruction to His disciples with the words "When you pray . . . ." He was saying, in effect, "Of course you are going to be praying on a regular basis."

Other Bible Examples

Jesus was not the only Bible example of people who prayed regularly. David said to God, "In the morning I lay my requests before you" (Psalm 5:3). For me personally, morning is the best time. That's because I am a morning person. Select a schedule most appropriate for you. David also prayed "evening . . . and noon" (Psalm 55:17). Little wonder there was so much power in his life!

Daniel was another who prayed regularly. Even when he was under a death threat for doing so, he went to his upstairs room that faced in the direction of Jerusalem and "three times a day he got down on his knees and prayed, giving thanks to his God" (Daniel 6:10). The Scriptures add the words "just as he had done before." Clearly Daniel was following a long-established pattern. He prayed regularly.

Prayer Requires Will Power

How does a person begin to pray regularly? By sheer will power. J. Sidlow Baxter, pastor, author and conference speaker, in his inimitable way relates his struggle to establish a regular prayer time.

"I looked at my watch," he writes, "and it said, 'Time for prayer, Sid.' But I looked at my desk and there was a miniature mountain of correspondence. And conscience said, 'You ought to answer those letters.' So, as we say in Scotland, I 'swithered.' I vacillated. Shall it be prayer, shall it be letters? Prayer? Letters?"

As Baxter "swithered," he had to admit that part of him did not want to pray. It was a contest between intellect and will on the one hand and emotions and fleshly desires on the other. Baxter continues: "I said to my will, 'Will, are you ready for prayer?' . . . So Will and I set off to pray." But not without a vicious struggle with emotions. The whole hour and a half was a fight.

But with each succeeding day, the struggle eased. And the morning finally came when, as Baxter expresses it, "While Will and I were pressing our case at the throne of the heavenly glory, one of the chief emotions shouted, 'Amen!' And for the first time the whole territory of J. Sidlow Baxter was happily coordinated in the exercise of prayer. God suddenly became real. Heaven was wide open, and Christ was there. The Holy Spirit was moving, and I knew that all the time God had been listening."

Conclusion

The validity and effectiveness of prayer are not determined by the subjective psychological condition of the one who prays. The thing that makes prayer valid and vital is this: faith takes hold of God's truth. That is all that is necessary.

Soon we shall be in the presence of the One who died for us, the One who redeemed us by His atoning blood. When you finally meet your Savior, don't you want to be able to say, "At last I'm seeing face to face the One who for years I have known heart to heart!"?

Resolve now that from this time on you will be a praying Christian. You will never, never, never, never regret it. Never!

Rev. Richard Sipley is a minister at large for The Christian and Missionary Alliance in Canada. He is also an associate evangelist for the Canadian Revival Fellowship and resides in Regina, Saskatchewan.